5 Full Length ISEE Lower Level Math Prac

www.EffortlessMath.com

... So Much More Online!

✓ FREE Math lessons

✓ More Math learning books!

✓ Mathematics Worksheets

✓ Online Math Tutors

Need a PDF version of this book?

Visit www.EffortlessMath.com

5 Full Length ISEE Lower Level Math Practice Tests

The Practice You Need to Ace the ISEE

Lower Level Math Test

By

Reza Nazari & Ava Ross

Copyright © 2019

Reza Nazari & Ava Ross

All rights reserved. No part of this publication may be reproduced, stored in a retrieval system, or transmitted in any form or by any means, electronic, mechanical, photocopying, recording, scanning, or otherwise, except as permitted under Section 107 or 108 of the 1976 United States Copyright Ac, without permission of the author.

All inquiries should be addressed to:

info@EffortlessMath.com

www.EffortlessMath.com

ISBN-13: 978-1-64612-119-9

ISBN-10: 1-64612-119-8

Published by: Effortless Math Education

www.EffortlessMath.com

Description

5 Full-Length ISEE Lower Level Math Practice Tests, which reflects the 2019 and 2020 test guidelines and topics, is designed to help you hone your math skills, overcome your exam anxiety, and boost your confidence -- and do your best to ace the ISEE Lower Level Math Test. The realistic and full-length ISEE Lower Level Math tests show you how the test is structured and what math topics you need to master. The practice test questions are followed by answer explanations to help you find your weak areas, learn from your mistakes, and raise your ISEE Lower Level Math score.

The surest way to succeed on ISEE Lower Level Math Test is with intensive practice in every math topic tested-- and that's what you will get in *5 Full-Length ISEE Lower Level Math Practice Tests*. This ISEE Lower Level Math new edition has been updated to replicate questions appearing on the most recent ISEE Lower Level Math tests. This is a precious learning tool for ISEE Lower Level test takers who need extra practice in math to improve their ISEE Lower Level Math score. After taking the ISEE Lower Level Math practice tests in this book, you will have solid foundation and adequate practice that is necessary to succeed on the ISEE Lower Level Math test. **This book is your ticket to ace the ISEE Lower Level Math Test!**

5 Full-Length ISEE Lower Level Math Practice Tests contains many exciting and unique features to help you improve your test scores, including:

- Content 100% aligned with the 2019 - 2020 ISEE Lower Level Math test

- Written by ISEE Math tutors and test experts

- Complete coverage of all ISEE Lower Level Math concepts and topics which you will be tested

- Detailed answers and explanations for every ISEE Lower Level Math practice questions to help you learn from your mistakes

- 5 full-length practice tests (featuring new question types) with detailed answers

This ISEE Lower Level Math book and other Effortless Math Education books are used by thousands of students each year to help them review core content areas, brush-up in math, discover their strengths and weaknesses, and achieve their best scores on the ISEE Lower Level Math test.

Contents

Description... 4

ISEE Lower Level Test Review.. 6

ISEE LOWER Level Math Practice Test 1... 8

ISEE LOWER Level Math Practice Test 2... 25

ISEE LOWER Level Math Practice Test 3... 42

ISEE LOWER Level Math Practice Test 4... 59

ISEE LOWER Level Math Practice Test 5... 76

ISEE Lower Level Math Practice Tests Answers and Explanations.................................. 92

ISEE Lower Level Test Review

The Independent School Entrance Exam (ISEE) is an admission test developed by the Educational Records Bureau for its member schools as part of their admission process.

ISEE Lower Level tests use a multiple-choice format and contain two Mathematics sections:

Quantitative Reasoning

There are 38 questions in the Quantitative Reasoning section and students have 35 minutes to answer the questions. This section contains word problems requiring either no calculation or simple calculation.

Mathematics Achievement

There are 30 questions in the Mathematics Achievement section and students have 30 minutes to answer the questions. Mathematics Achievement measures students' knowledge of Mathematics requiring one or more steps in calculating the answer.

In this book, there are five complete ISEE Lower Level Quantitative Reasoning and Mathematics Achievement practice tests. Take these tests to see what score you'll be able to receive on a real ISEE Lower Level test.

Good luck!

Time to Test

Time to refine your skill with a practice examination

Take a practice ISEE Lower Level Math Test to simulate the test day experience. After you've finished, score your test using the answer key.

Before You Start

- You'll need a pencil and scratch papers to take the test.
- For each question, there are four possible answers. Choose which one is best.
- It's okay to guess. You won't lose any points if you're wrong.
- Use the answer sheet provided to record your answers.
- After you've finished the test, review the answer key to see where you went wrong.
- **Calculators are NOT allowed for the ISEE Lower Level Test.**

Good Luck

ISEE LOWER Level Math Practice Test 1

2019 - 2020

Two Parts

Total number of questions: 68

Quantitative Reasoning: 38 questions

Mathematics Achievement: 30 questions

Total time for two parts: 65 Minutes

ISEE Lower Level Practice Test Answer Sheets

Remove (or photocopy) these answer sheets and use them to complete the practice tests.

ISEE Lower Level Practice Test 1

Quantitative Reasoning | Mathematics Achievement

#	Q.R.	#	Q.R.	#	M.A.	#	M.A.
1	Ⓐ Ⓑ Ⓒ Ⓓ	21	Ⓐ Ⓑ Ⓒ Ⓓ	1	Ⓐ Ⓑ Ⓒ Ⓓ	21	Ⓐ Ⓑ Ⓒ Ⓓ
2	Ⓐ Ⓑ Ⓒ Ⓓ	22	Ⓐ Ⓑ Ⓒ Ⓓ	2	Ⓐ Ⓑ Ⓒ Ⓓ	22	Ⓐ Ⓑ Ⓒ Ⓓ
3	Ⓐ Ⓑ Ⓒ Ⓓ	23	Ⓐ Ⓑ Ⓒ Ⓓ	3	Ⓐ Ⓑ Ⓒ Ⓓ	23	Ⓐ Ⓑ Ⓒ Ⓓ
4	Ⓐ Ⓑ Ⓒ Ⓓ	24	Ⓐ Ⓑ Ⓒ Ⓓ	4	Ⓐ Ⓑ Ⓒ Ⓓ	24	Ⓐ Ⓑ Ⓒ Ⓓ
5	Ⓐ Ⓑ Ⓒ Ⓓ	25	Ⓐ Ⓑ Ⓒ Ⓓ	5	Ⓐ Ⓑ Ⓒ Ⓓ	25	Ⓐ Ⓑ Ⓒ Ⓓ
6	Ⓐ Ⓑ Ⓒ Ⓓ	26	Ⓐ Ⓑ Ⓒ Ⓓ	6	Ⓐ Ⓑ Ⓒ Ⓓ	26	Ⓐ Ⓑ Ⓒ Ⓓ
7	Ⓐ Ⓑ Ⓒ Ⓓ	27	Ⓐ Ⓑ Ⓒ Ⓓ	7	Ⓐ Ⓑ Ⓒ Ⓓ	27	Ⓐ Ⓑ Ⓒ Ⓓ
8	Ⓐ Ⓑ Ⓒ Ⓓ	28	Ⓐ Ⓑ Ⓒ Ⓓ	8	Ⓐ Ⓑ Ⓒ Ⓓ	28	Ⓐ Ⓑ Ⓒ Ⓓ
9	Ⓐ Ⓑ Ⓒ Ⓓ	29	Ⓐ Ⓑ Ⓒ Ⓓ	9	Ⓐ Ⓑ Ⓒ Ⓓ	29	Ⓐ Ⓑ Ⓒ Ⓓ
10	Ⓐ Ⓑ Ⓒ Ⓓ	30	Ⓐ Ⓑ Ⓒ Ⓓ	10	Ⓐ Ⓑ Ⓒ Ⓓ	30	Ⓐ Ⓑ Ⓒ Ⓓ
11	Ⓐ Ⓑ Ⓒ Ⓓ	31	Ⓐ Ⓑ Ⓒ Ⓓ	11	Ⓐ Ⓑ Ⓒ Ⓓ		
12	Ⓐ Ⓑ Ⓒ Ⓓ	32	Ⓐ Ⓑ Ⓒ Ⓓ	12	Ⓐ Ⓑ Ⓒ Ⓓ		
13	Ⓐ Ⓑ Ⓒ Ⓓ	33	Ⓐ Ⓑ Ⓒ Ⓓ	13	Ⓐ Ⓑ Ⓒ Ⓓ		
14	Ⓐ Ⓑ Ⓒ Ⓓ	34	Ⓐ Ⓑ Ⓒ Ⓓ	14	Ⓐ Ⓑ Ⓒ Ⓓ		
15	Ⓐ Ⓑ Ⓒ Ⓓ	35	Ⓐ Ⓑ Ⓒ Ⓓ	15	Ⓐ Ⓑ Ⓒ Ⓓ		
16	Ⓐ Ⓑ Ⓒ Ⓓ	36	Ⓐ Ⓑ Ⓒ Ⓓ	16	Ⓐ Ⓑ Ⓒ Ⓓ		
17	Ⓐ Ⓑ Ⓒ Ⓓ	37	Ⓐ Ⓑ Ⓒ Ⓓ	17	Ⓐ Ⓑ Ⓒ Ⓓ		
18	Ⓐ Ⓑ Ⓒ Ⓓ	38	Ⓐ Ⓑ Ⓒ Ⓓ	18	Ⓐ Ⓑ Ⓒ Ⓓ		
19	Ⓐ Ⓑ Ⓒ Ⓓ			19	Ⓐ Ⓑ Ⓒ Ⓓ		
20	Ⓐ Ⓑ Ⓒ Ⓓ			20	Ⓐ Ⓑ Ⓒ Ⓓ		

ISEE Lower Level Practice Test 1

Quantitative Reasoning

38 questions

Total time for this test: 35 Minutes

You may NOT use a calculator for this test.

1) Which of the following is greater than $\frac{14}{8}$?
A. $\frac{1}{2}$
B. $\frac{5}{2}$
C. $\frac{4}{3}$
D. 1.5

2) If $\frac{1}{3}$ of a number is greater than 9, the number must be .....
A. Less than 4
B. Equal to 15
C. Equal to 27
D. Greater than 27

3) If $5 \times (M + N) = 25$ and M is greater than 0, then N could Not be .....
A. 1
B. 2
C. 3
D. 5

4) Which of the following is closest to 4.03?
A. 5
B. 4.5
C. 4
D. 3.9

5) At a Zoo, the ratio of lions to tigers is 12 to 4. Which of the following could NOT be the total number of lions and tigers in the zoo?
A. 32
B. 64
C. 98
D. 112

6) In the multiplication bellow, A represents which digit?
$$12 \times 3A2 = 4,104$$
A. 2
B. 3
C. 4
D. 6

7) If M is an even number, which of the following is always an odd number?
   A. $\frac{M}{2}$
   B. $M + 4$
   C. $4M$
   D. $M + 3$

8) $9.9 - 5.08$ is closest to which of the following.
   A. 4.1
   B. 4.8
   C. 6
   D. 8

$$x = 3{,}426 \qquad y = 329$$

9) Numbers x and y are shown above. How many times larger is the value of digit 2 in the number x, than the value of digit 5 in the number y?
   A. 1
   B. 10
   C. 100
   D. 1,000

10) If 5 added to a number, the sum is 20. If the same number added to 35, the answer is
   A. 30
   B. 45
   C. 50
   D. 55

11) $\dfrac{2+5+6\times 1+1}{6+2} = ?$
   A. $\dfrac{15}{8}$
   B. $\dfrac{4}{8}$
   C. $\dfrac{7}{4}$
   D. $\dfrac{6}{8}$

12) $7 \times 4 \times 12 \times 3$ is equal to the product of 28 and
   A. 3
   B. 12
   C. 24
   D. 36

13) If 20 is the product of 5 and x, then 20 can be divided by which of the following?
A. $x + 4$
B. $2x - 4$
C. $x - 1$
D. $x \times 4$

14) Use the equations below to answer the question:
$$x + 12 = 18$$
$$17 + y = 21$$
What is the value of $x + y$?

A. 8
B. 9
C. 10
D. 12

15) Which of the following expressions has the same value as $\frac{2}{5} \times \frac{10}{4}$?
A. $\frac{2 \times 4}{4}$
B. $\frac{2 \times 5}{20}$
C. $\frac{5 \times 6}{4}$
D. $\frac{5 \times 4}{20}$

16) When 5 is added to three times number N, the result is 50. Then N is ….
A. 11
B. 15
C. 16
D. 18

17) At noon, the temperature was 15 degrees. By midnight, it had dropped another 25 degrees. What was the temperature at midnight?
A. 5 $degrees\ above\ zero$
B. 5 $degrees\ below\ zero$
C. 10 $degrees\ above\ zero$
D. 10 $degrees\ below\ zero$

18) If a triangle has a base of 6 cm and a height of 9 cm, what is the area of the triangle?
A. $25\ cm^2$
B. $27\ cm^2$
C. $40\ cm^2$
D. $54\ cm^2$

19) Which formula would you use to find the area of a triangle?
A. $length \times width \times height$
B. $\frac{1}{2} base \times height$
C. $length \times width$
D. $side \times side$

20) What is the next number in this sequence?   3, 6, 10, 15, 21, ...
A. 28
B. 27
C. 25
D. 24

21) What is the average of the following numbers?   7, 11, 12, 23, 45
A. 19.2
B. 19.6
C. 19.8
D. 20

22) If there are 8 red balls and 16 blue balls in a basket, what is the probability that John will pick out a red ball from the basket?
A. $\frac{16}{8}$
B. $\frac{1}{3}$
C. $\frac{2}{10}$
D. $\frac{3}{5}$

23) A square has a perimeter of 24. What is the length of one side?
A. 3
B. 4
C. 6
D. 8

24) What is %10 of 300?
A. 10
B. 30
C. 35
D. 40

25) Which of the following statement is False?
A. $3 \times 3 = 9$
B. $(4 + 1) \times 5 = 25$
C. $6 \div (4 - 1) = 1$
D. $6 \times (4 - 2) = 12$

26) If all the sides in the following figure are of equal length and length of one side is 5, what is the perimeter of the figure?
A. 15
B. 20
C. 25
D. 30

27) $\frac{4}{5} - \frac{2}{5} = ?$
A. 0.3
B. 0.35
C. 0.4
D. 0.45

28) If $N = 2$ and $\frac{64}{N} + 8 = \square$, then $\square$ = ...
A. 30
B. 32
C. 36
D. 40

29) Which of the following is not equal to $\frac{1}{3}$?
A. $\frac{2}{6}$
B. $\frac{3}{9}$
C. $\frac{5}{15}$
D. $\frac{8}{21}$

30) What is the median of these numbers? 3, 10, 13, 8, 15, 19, 5
A. 8
B. 10
C. 13
D. 15

The result of a research shows the number of men and women in four cities of a country.

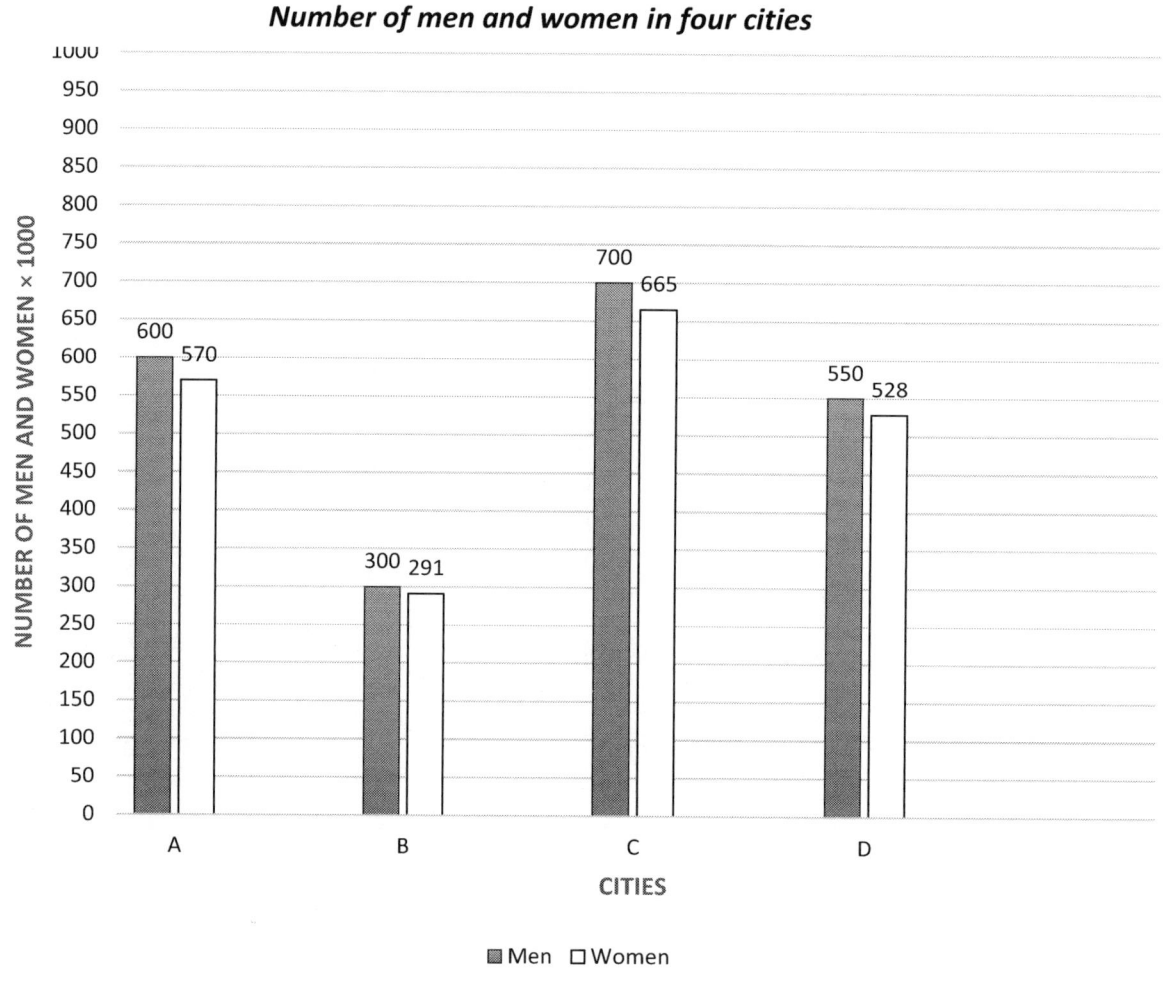

31) What is the difference of the population of men in the biggest city and in the smallest city?
A. 200
B. 300
C. 400
D. 500

32) What is 4,231.48245 rounded to the nearest tenth?

A. 4,231.482
B. 4,231.5
C. 4,231
D. 4,231.48

33) $18a + 32 = 50, a = ?$
A. 1
B. 4
C. 11
D. 12

34) Two angles of a triangle measure 30 and 65. What is the measure of third angle?
A. 50
B. 60
C. 70
D. 85

35) A woman weighs 145 pounds. She gains 15 pounds one month and 9 pounds the next month. What is her new weight?
A. 142 Pounds
B. 146 Pounds
C. 169 Pounds
D. 178 Pounds

36) In a basket, there are equal numbers of red, white, yellow, and purple cards. Which of the following could be the number of cards in the basket?
A. 123
B. 82
C. 66
D. 56

37) Jim types 88 words per minute. How many words does he type in 15 seconds?
A. 15
B. 18
C. 22
D. 25

38) Which of the following is NOT equal to $\frac{2}{7}$?
A. $\frac{22}{77}$
B. $\frac{8}{28}$
C. $\frac{18}{63}$
D. $\frac{12}{48}$

IF YOU FINISH BEFORE TIME IS CALLED, YOU MAY CHECK YOUR WORK ON THIS SECTION ONLY. DO NOT TURN TO ANY OTHER SECTION IN THE TEST. **STOP**

ISEE Lower Level Practice Test 1

Mathematics Achievement

30 questions

Total time for this test: 30 Minutes

You may NOT use a calculator for this test.

1) $\frac{1}{5} + \frac{3}{4} =$

A. $\frac{4}{9}$
B. $\frac{3}{9}$
C. $\frac{3}{4}$
D. $\frac{19}{20}$

2) What's the least common multiple (LCM) of 6 and 16?

A. 6 and 16 have no common multiples
B. 112
C. 96
D. 48

3) Which of the following is NOT a factor of 45?

A. 3
B. 5
C. 9
D. 12

4) While at work, Emma checks her email once every 80 minutes. In 8-hour, how many times does she check her email?

A. 3 $Times$
B. 4 $Times$
C. 5 $Times$
D. 6 $Times$

5) What is 2,923.2769 rounded to the nearest tenth?

A. 2,923.3
B. 2,923.277
C. 2,923
D. 2,923.27

6) Which of the following fractions is the largest?

A. $\frac{3}{4}$
B. $\frac{1}{5}$
C. $\frac{8}{9}$
D. $\frac{2}{3}$

7) A bag contains 18 balls: two green, five black, eight blue, a brown, a red and one white. If 17 balls are removed from the bag at random, what is the probability that a brown ball has been removed?

A. $\frac{1}{9}$

B. $\frac{1}{6}$

C. $\frac{16}{17}$

D. $\frac{17}{18}$

8) From last year, the price of gasoline has increased from $1.40 per gallon to $1.75 per gallon. The new price is what percent of the original price?

A. 72%
B. 115%
C. 125%
D. 160%

9) Emma purchased a computer for $504. The computer is regularly priced at $600. What was the percent discount Emma received on the computer?

A. 12%
B. 16%
C. 18%
D. 25%

10) In the given diagram, the height is 6 cm. what is the area of the triangle?

A. $23 cm^2$
B. $46\ cm^2$
C. $78\ cm^2$
D. $152\ cm^2$

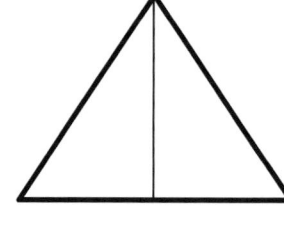

26 cm

11) Two angles of a triangle measure 50 and 45. What is the measure of the third angle?

A. 85
B. 95
C. 102
D. 262

12) If a rectangular swimming pool has a perimeter of 112 feet and is 22 feet wide, what is its area?

A. 1,496
B. 900
C. 840
D. 748

13) Mike is 8.5 miles ahead of Julia running at 6.5 miles per hour and Julia is running at the speed of 7 miles per hour. How long does it take Julia to catch Mike?

A. 2 $hours$
B. 5.5 $hours$
C. 8.5 $hours$
D. 17 $hours$

14) Julie gives 6 pieces of candy to each of her friends. If Julie gives all her candy away, which amount of candy could have been the amount she distributed?

A. 180
B. 217
C. 243
D. 263

15) A taxi driver earns $8 per 1-hour work. If he works 10 hours a day and in 1 hour he uses 2-liters petrol with price $1 for 1-liter. How much money does he earn in one day?

A. $90
B. $78
C. $60
D. $50

16) Convert 0.035 to a percent.

A. 0.03%
B. 0.35%
C. 3.50%
D. 35%

17) The number 0.03 can also represented by which of the following?

A. $\frac{3}{10}$
B. $\frac{3}{100}$
C. $\frac{3}{1,000}$
D. $\frac{3}{10,000}$

18) The width of a box is one third of its length. The height of the box is half of its width. If the length of the box is 24 cm, what is the volume of the box?
A. 81 cm^3
B. 162 cm^3
C. 243 cm^3
D. 768 cm^3

19) 125 students took an exam and 20 of them failed. What percent of the students passed the exam?
A. 20%
B. 50%
C. 60%
D. 84%

20) $\begin{array}{r} 25 \text{ hr. } 25 \text{ min.} \\ - 23 \text{ hr. } 38 \text{ min.} \\ \hline \end{array}$

A. 1 hr. 57 min.
B. 1 hr. 53 min.
C. 1 hr. 47 min.
D. 2 hr. 17 min.

21) Which of the following is an obtuse angle?

A. 129°
B. 85°
C. 78°
D. 25°

Use the following table to answer question below.

DANIEL'S BIRD-WATCHING PROJECT	
DAY	NUMBER OF RAPTORS SEEN
Monday	?
Tuesday	9
Wednesday	14
Thursday	12
Friday	5
MEAN	20

22) This table shows the data Daniel collects while watching birds for one week. How many raptors did Daniel see on Monday?
A. 60
B. 51
C. 42
D. 33

23) In the following figure, the shaded squares are what fractional part of the whole set of squares?

A. $\frac{1}{2}$
B. $\frac{5}{8}$
C. $\frac{2}{3}$
D. $\frac{8}{15}$

24) If a box contains red and blue balls in ratio of 2 : 3 red to blue, how many red balls are there if 60 blue balls are in the box?
A. 30
B. 40
C. 60
D. 82

25) A shirt costing $700 is discounted 15%. After a month, the shirt is discounted another 15%. Which of the following expressions can be used to find the selling price of the shirt?
A. $(700)(0.70)$
B. $(700) - 700(0.30)$
C. $(700)(0.15) - (700)(0.15)$
D. $(700)(0.85)(0.85)$

26) Emma draws a shape that has four equal sides on her paper. All sides and angles of the shape are equal. What shape does Emma draw?
A. Parallelogram
B. Rectangle
C. Trapezoid
D. Square

27) If $A = 30$, then which of the following equations are correct?
A. $A + 20 = 50$
B. $A \div 20 = 50$
C. $20 \times A = 50$
D. $A - 20 = 50$

28) Joe makes $4.75 per hour at his work. If he works 7 hours, how much money will he earn?
A. $22.00
B. $24.75
C. $31.50
D. $33.25

29) In a classroom of 44 students, 20 are male. About what percentage of the class is female?
A. 63%
B. 61%
C. 59%
D. 55%

30) Nancy ordered 17 pizzas. Each pizza has 8 slices. How many slices of pizza did Nancy ordered?
A. 124
B. 136
C. 158
D. 180

IF YOU FINISH BEFORE TIME IS CALLED, YOU MAY CHECK YOUR WORK ON THIS SECTION ONLY. DO NOT TURN TO ANY OTHER SECTION IN THE TEST. **STOP**

ISEE LOWER Level Math Practice Test 2

2019 - 2020

Two Parts

Total number of questions: 68

Quantitative Reasoning: 38 questions

Mathematics Achievement: 30 questions

Total time for two parts: 65 Minutes

ISEE Lower Level Practice Test Answer Sheets

Remove (or photocopy) these answer sheets and use them to complete the practice tests.

ISEE Lower Level Practice Test 2

Quantitative Reasoning		Mathematics Achievement	
1 Ⓐ Ⓑ Ⓒ Ⓓ	21 Ⓐ Ⓑ Ⓒ Ⓓ	1 Ⓐ Ⓑ Ⓒ Ⓓ	21 Ⓐ Ⓑ Ⓒ Ⓓ
2 Ⓐ Ⓑ Ⓒ Ⓓ	22 Ⓐ Ⓑ Ⓒ Ⓓ	2 Ⓐ Ⓑ Ⓒ Ⓓ	22 Ⓐ Ⓑ Ⓒ Ⓓ
3 Ⓐ Ⓑ Ⓒ Ⓓ	23 Ⓐ Ⓑ Ⓒ Ⓓ	3 Ⓐ Ⓑ Ⓒ Ⓓ	23 Ⓐ Ⓑ Ⓒ Ⓓ
4 Ⓐ Ⓑ Ⓒ Ⓓ	24 Ⓐ Ⓑ Ⓒ Ⓓ	4 Ⓐ Ⓑ Ⓒ Ⓓ	24 Ⓐ Ⓑ Ⓒ Ⓓ
5 Ⓐ Ⓑ Ⓒ Ⓓ	25 Ⓐ Ⓑ Ⓒ Ⓓ	5 Ⓐ Ⓑ Ⓒ Ⓓ	25 Ⓐ Ⓑ Ⓒ Ⓓ
6 Ⓐ Ⓑ Ⓒ Ⓓ	26 Ⓐ Ⓑ Ⓒ Ⓓ	6 Ⓐ Ⓑ Ⓒ Ⓓ	26 Ⓐ Ⓑ Ⓒ Ⓓ
7 Ⓐ Ⓑ Ⓒ Ⓓ	27 Ⓐ Ⓑ Ⓒ Ⓓ	7 Ⓐ Ⓑ Ⓒ Ⓓ	27 Ⓐ Ⓑ Ⓒ Ⓓ
8 Ⓐ Ⓑ Ⓒ Ⓓ	28 Ⓐ Ⓑ Ⓒ Ⓓ	8 Ⓐ Ⓑ Ⓒ Ⓓ	28 Ⓐ Ⓑ Ⓒ Ⓓ
9 Ⓐ Ⓑ Ⓒ Ⓓ	29 Ⓐ Ⓑ Ⓒ Ⓓ	9 Ⓐ Ⓑ Ⓒ Ⓓ	29 Ⓐ Ⓑ Ⓒ Ⓓ
10 Ⓐ Ⓑ Ⓒ Ⓓ	30 Ⓐ Ⓑ Ⓒ Ⓓ	10 Ⓐ Ⓑ Ⓒ Ⓓ	30 Ⓐ Ⓑ Ⓒ Ⓓ
11 Ⓐ Ⓑ Ⓒ Ⓓ	31 Ⓐ Ⓑ Ⓒ Ⓓ	11 Ⓐ Ⓑ Ⓒ Ⓓ	
12 Ⓐ Ⓑ Ⓒ Ⓓ	32 Ⓐ Ⓑ Ⓒ Ⓓ	12 Ⓐ Ⓑ Ⓒ Ⓓ	
13 Ⓐ Ⓑ Ⓒ Ⓓ	33 Ⓐ Ⓑ Ⓒ Ⓓ	13 Ⓐ Ⓑ Ⓒ Ⓓ	
14 Ⓐ Ⓑ Ⓒ Ⓓ	34 Ⓐ Ⓑ Ⓒ Ⓓ	14 Ⓐ Ⓑ Ⓒ Ⓓ	
15 Ⓐ Ⓑ Ⓒ Ⓓ	35 Ⓐ Ⓑ Ⓒ Ⓓ	15 Ⓐ Ⓑ Ⓒ Ⓓ	
16 Ⓐ Ⓑ Ⓒ Ⓓ	36 Ⓐ Ⓑ Ⓒ Ⓓ	16 Ⓐ Ⓑ Ⓒ Ⓓ	
17 Ⓐ Ⓑ Ⓒ Ⓓ	37 Ⓐ Ⓑ Ⓒ Ⓓ	17 Ⓐ Ⓑ Ⓒ Ⓓ	
18 Ⓐ Ⓑ Ⓒ Ⓓ	38 Ⓐ Ⓑ Ⓒ Ⓓ	18 Ⓐ Ⓑ Ⓒ Ⓓ	
19 Ⓐ Ⓑ Ⓒ Ⓓ		19 Ⓐ Ⓑ Ⓒ Ⓓ	
20 Ⓐ Ⓑ Ⓒ Ⓓ		20 Ⓐ Ⓑ Ⓒ Ⓓ	

ISEE Lower Level Practice Test 2

Quantitative Reasoning

38 questions

Total time for this test: 35 Minutes

You may NOT use a calculator for this test.

1) $\frac{10}{2} - \frac{3}{2} = ?$
A. 1
B. 2.5
C. 3
D. 3.5

2) If $58 = 2 \times N + 12$, then $N = ...$
A. 18
B. 23
C. 24
D. 35

3) When 3 is added to four times a number N, the result is 24. Which of the following equations represents this statement?
A. $4 + 3N = 24$
B. $24N + 4 = 3$
C. $4N + 3 = 24$
D. $4N + 24 = 3$

4) When 105 is divided by 6, the remainder is the same as when 87 is divided by
A. 8
B. 6
C. 5
D. 4

5) John has 2,400 cards and Max has 506 cards. How many more cards does John have than Max?
A. 1,894
B. 2,798
C. 2,812
D. 2,828

6) In the following right triangle, what is the value of x?
A. 15
B. 30
C. 45
D. 60

7) What is 5 percent of 360?
A. 10
B. 18
C. 20
D. 40

8) In a basket, the ratio of red marbles to blue marbles is 5 to 1. Which of the following could NOT be the total number of red and blue marbles in the basket?
   A. 18
   B. 26
   C. 54
   D. 60

9) A square has an area of $64 cm^2$. What is its perimeter?
   A. 28 cm
   B. 32 cm
   C. 34 cm
   D. 36 cm

10) Find the missing number in the sequence: $6, 9, 13, \ldots, 24$
    A. 15
    B. 18
    C. 19
    D. 20

11) The length of a rectangle is 3 times of its width. If the length is 24, what is the perimeter of the rectangle?
    A. 24
    B. 30
    C. 48
    D. 64

12) Mary has M dollars. John has $10 more than Mary. If John gives Mary $13, then in terms of M, how much does John have now?
    A. $M + 1$
    B. $M + 10$
    C. $M - 3$
    D. $M - 1$

13) Dividing 215 by 6 leaves a remainder of
    A. 1
    B. 2
    C. 3
    D. 5

14) If $6,000 + A - 400 = 8,400$, then $A =$
A. 200
B. 1600
C. 2,800
D. 2,900

15) For what price is 12 percent off the same as $90 off?
A. $200
B. $300
C. $450
D. $750

16) Which of the following fractions is less than $\frac{5}{2}$?
A. 2.4
B. $\frac{7}{2}$
C. 3
D. 3.8

17) Use the equation below to answer the question.
$$x + 4 = 7$$
$$2y = 10$$
What is the value of $y - x$?
A. 1
B. 2
C. 3
D. 4

18) If $320 - x + 216 = 425$, then $x = ?$
A. 101
B. 106
C. 111
D. 221

19) Of the following, 25 percent of $53.99 is closest to
A. $9.90
B. $11.00
C. $13.50
D. $14.50

20) Solve.
$$9.08 - 5.6 = \ldots$$
A. 2.42
B. 2.46
C. 3.48
D. 3.55

21) If $600 + \square - 180 = 1{,}200$, then $\square = ?$
A. 580
B. 660
C. 700
D. 780

22) There are 60 students in a class. If the ratio of the number of girls to the total number of students in the class is $\frac{1}{5}$, which of the following is the number of boys in that class?
A. 10
B. 20
C. 25
D. 48

23) If $N \times (6 - 4) = 14$ then $N = ?$
A. 7
B. 12
C. 13
D. 14

24) If $x \blacksquare y = 4x + y - 2$, what is the value of $4 \blacksquare 16$?
A. 14
B. 28
C. 30
D. 36

25) Of the following, which number if the greatest?
A. 0.092
B. 0.9913
C. 0.9923
D. 0.9896

26) $\frac{9}{8} - \frac{3}{4} = ?$
A. 0.125
B. 0.375
C. 0.5
D. 0.625

27) Which of the following is the closest to 5.02?
A. 5
B. 5.2
C. 5.3
D. 5.5

28) Which of the following statements is False?
A. $(7 \times 3 + 14) \times 2 = 70$
B. $(2 \times 5 + 4) \div 7 = 2$
C. $3 + (3 \times 6) = 21$
D. $14 \div (4 + 3) = 3$

29) A trash container, when empty, weighs 38 pounds. If this container is filled with a load of trash that weighs 250 pounds, what is the total weight of the container and its contents?

A. 224 pounds
B. 288 pounds
C. 295 pounds
D. 325 pounds

30) During the six-month period shown, what is the median number of shoes per month?
A. 25
B. 30
C. 35
D. 40

31) A writer finishes 270 pages of his manuscript in 30 hours. How many pages is his average?

A. 18
B. 15
C. 10
D. 9

32) The distance between cities A and B is approximately 3,400 miles. If Nicole drives an average of 50 miles per hour, how many hours will it take her to drive from city A to city B?

A. *approximately* 70 *hours*
B. *approximately* 68 *hours*
C. *approximately* 49 *hours*
D. *approximately* 27 *hours*

33) $\frac{14}{35}$ is equal to:

A. 5.2
B. 0.46
C. 0.4
D. 0.33

34) $10a + 30 = 140, a = ?$

A. 10
B. 11
C. 14
D. 18

35) What is the place value of 1 in 6.7315?

A. Hundredths
B. Thousandths
C. Ten thousandths
D. Hundred thousandths

36) Which of the following is NOT a prime factor of 70?
A. 2
B. 5
C. 7
D. 9

37) Which of these numbers is equal to $\frac{25}{1,000}$?

A. 2.5
B. 0.25
C. 0.025
D. 0.0025

38) During a 18-hour day, Moe works $\frac{1}{3}$ of the time. How many hours does Moe work in that day?

A. 2 *hours*
B. 4 *hours*
C. 5 *hours*
D. 6 *hours*

IF YOU FINISH BEFORE TIME IS CALLED, YOU MAY CHECK YOUR WORK ON THIS SECTION ONLY. DO NOT TURN TO ANY OTHER SECTION IN THE TEST. **STOP**

ISEE Lower Level Practice Test 2

Mathematics Achievement

30 questions

Total time for this test: 30 Minutes

You may NOT use a calculator for this test.

1) Which is seventy-four thousand, eight hundred nineteen?

A. 74,819
B. 740,819
C. 704,819
D. 748,019

2) $300 + 950 =$

A. 1,050
B. 1,150
C. 1,250
D. 1,400

3) Which of the following is not a multiple of 7?

A. 12
B. 14
C. 28
D. 56

4) A right triangle has sides with lengths 5, 12 and 13. What is the perimeter of the triangle?
A. 13
B. 18
C. 30
D. 36

5) What is the product of 11 and 5?
A. 0.115
B. 11.5
C. 16
D. 55

6) With what number must 6.674312 be multiplied in order to obtain the number 66,743.12?
A. 100
B. 1,000
C. 10,000
D. 100,000

7) Which expression is equal to $\frac{4}{13}$?
A. $4 - 13$
B. $4 \div 13$
C. 4×13
D. $\frac{13}{4}$

8) Lily and Ella are in a pancake–eating contest. Lily can eat two pancakes per minute, while Ella can eat $3\frac{1}{2}$ pancakes per minute. How many total pancakes can they eat in 5 minutes?
A. 9.5 Pancakes
B. 29.5 Pancakes
C. 27.5 Pancakes
D. 11.5 Pancakes

9) Which expression has a value of 18?
A. $8-(-2)+(-18)$
B. $2+(-3)\times(-2)$
C. $-6\times(-6)+(-2)\times(-12)$
D. $(-2)\times(-7)+4$

10) $0.79 + 1.5 + 3.23 = ?$

A. 2.5
B. 4.2
C. 5.52
D. 6.5

11) What is the perimeter of a rectangle that has a length of 6 inches and a width of 4 inches?
A. 10 in.
B. 20 in.
C. 26 in.
D. 28 in.

12) How many $\frac{1}{6}$ cup servings are in a package of cheese that contains $5\frac{1}{2}$ cups altogether?
A. 20
B. 22
C. 24
D. 33

13) If the following clock shows a time in the morning, what time was it 4 hours and 30 minutes ago?
A. 05:45 AM
B. 07:45 AM
C. 09:45 PM
D. 010:15 PM

14) The area of a rectangle is 54 square meters. The width is 6 meters. What is the length of the rectangle?
   A. 8
   B. 9
   C. 10
   D. 12

Use the table below to answer the question.

City Populations

City	Population
Denton	28,097
Bomberg	28,307
Windham	29,900
Sandhill	26,980

15) Which list of city populations is in order from least to greatest?

A. 28,097;	28,307;	29,900;	26,980
B. 29,900;	28,307;	28,097;	26,980
C. 26,980;	28,097;	28,307;	29,900
D. 26,980;	28,307;	28,097;	29,900

16) The temperature on Sunday at 12:00 PM was 77°F. Low temperature on the same day was 25°F cooler. Which temperature is closest to the low temperature on that day?
   A. 76°F
   B. 52°F
   C. 51°F
   D. 75°

17) $(9 + 5) \div (3^2 \div 3) =$ ___
   A. $\frac{5}{7}$
   B. 2
   C. 5
   D. 12

18) Ella buys five items costing $3.26, $15.69, $2.50, $4.66, and $17.99. What is the estimated total cost of Ella's items?
A. between $25 and $30
B. between $30 and $35
C. between $35 and $40
D. between $42 and $47

19) How long is the line segment shown on the number line below?
A. 6
B. 7
C. 8
D. 9

20) There are 87 students from Riddle Elementary school at the library on Monday. The other 43 students in the school are practicing in the classroom. Which number sentence shows the total number of students in Riddle Elementary school?
A. $87 + 43$
B. $87 - 43$
C. 87×43
D. $87 \div 43$

21) $\frac{12}{20}$ is equal to:
A. 0.60
B. 6.31
C. 63.10
D. 631.00

22) Which number correctly completes the number sentence $70 \times 36 = ?$
A. 372
B. 660
C. 1,920
D. 2,520

23) If $8 + a = 14$ and $4 + b = 12$, then what is the value of $a + b$?
A. 8
B. 12
C. 14
D. 16

24) Which statement about the number 749,382.16 is true?

A. *The digit 6 has a value of* (6×100)
B. *The digit 4 has a value of* (4×100)
C. *The digit 8 has a value of* (8×10)
D. *The digit 9 has a value of* (9×100)

25) Ella described a number using these clues:
   Three – digit odd numbers that have a 7 in the hundreds place and a 4 in the tens place
   Which number could fit Ella's description?
A. 727
B. 747
C. 742
D. 746

26) The following graph shows the mark of six students in mathematics. What is the mean (average) of the marks?

A. 15
B. 14.57
C. 14.3
D. 13.5

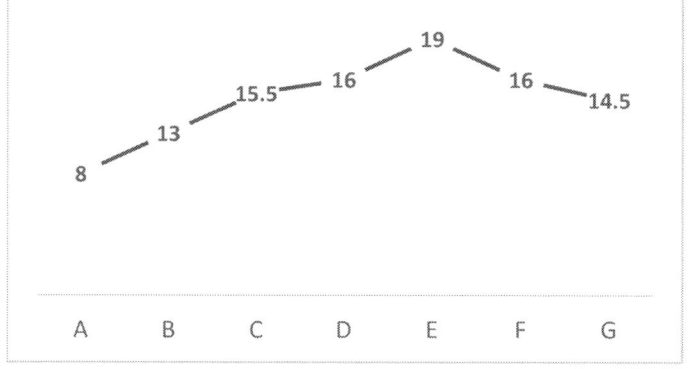

27) In the deck of cards, there are 4 spades, 3 hearts, 9 clubs, and 8 diamonds. What is the probability that William will pick out a spade?

A. $\frac{1}{6}$
B. $\frac{1}{8}$
C. $\frac{1}{9}$
D. $\frac{1}{5}$

28) Jason's favorite sports team has won 0.52 of its games this season. How can Jason express this decimal as a fraction?

A. $\dfrac{5}{2}$

B. $\dfrac{52}{10}$

C. $\dfrac{52}{100}$

D. $\dfrac{5.2}{10}$

29) Which fraction has the least value?

A. $\dfrac{1}{3}$

B. $\dfrac{3}{10}$

C. $\dfrac{2}{5}$

D. $\dfrac{11}{16}$

30) Which of the following is closest to 200.22?

A. 190
B. 199.5
C. 200
D. 200.3

IF YOU FINISH BEFORE TIME IS CALLED, YOU MAY CHECK YOUR WORK ON THIS SECTION ONLY. DO NOT TURN TO ANY OTHER SECTION IN THE TEST.

STOP

ISEE LOWER Level Math Practice Test 3

2019 - 2020

Two Parts

Total number of questions: 68

Quantitative Reasoning: 38 questions

Mathematics Achievement: 30 questions

Total time for two parts: 65 Minutes

ISEE Lower Level Practice Test Answer Sheets

Remove (or photocopy) these answer sheets and use them to complete the practice tests.

ISEE Lower Level Practice Test 3

Quantitative Reasoning | **Mathematics Achievement**

Quantitative Reasoning:
1. Ⓐ Ⓑ Ⓒ Ⓓ
2. Ⓐ Ⓑ Ⓒ Ⓓ
3. Ⓐ Ⓑ Ⓒ Ⓓ
4. Ⓐ Ⓑ Ⓒ Ⓓ
5. Ⓐ Ⓑ Ⓒ Ⓓ
6. Ⓐ Ⓑ Ⓒ Ⓓ
7. Ⓐ Ⓑ Ⓒ Ⓓ
8. Ⓐ Ⓑ Ⓒ Ⓓ
9. Ⓐ Ⓑ Ⓒ Ⓓ
10. Ⓐ Ⓑ Ⓒ Ⓓ
11. Ⓐ Ⓑ Ⓒ Ⓓ
12. Ⓐ Ⓑ Ⓒ Ⓓ
13. Ⓐ Ⓑ Ⓒ Ⓓ
14. Ⓐ Ⓑ Ⓒ Ⓓ
15. Ⓐ Ⓑ Ⓒ Ⓓ
16. Ⓐ Ⓑ Ⓒ Ⓓ
17. Ⓐ Ⓑ Ⓒ Ⓓ
18. Ⓐ Ⓑ Ⓒ Ⓓ
19. Ⓐ Ⓑ Ⓒ Ⓓ
20. Ⓐ Ⓑ Ⓒ Ⓓ
21. Ⓐ Ⓑ Ⓒ Ⓓ
22. Ⓐ Ⓑ Ⓒ Ⓓ
23. Ⓐ Ⓑ Ⓒ Ⓓ
24. Ⓐ Ⓑ Ⓒ Ⓓ
25. Ⓐ Ⓑ Ⓒ Ⓓ
26. Ⓐ Ⓑ Ⓒ Ⓓ
27. Ⓐ Ⓑ Ⓒ Ⓓ
28. Ⓐ Ⓑ Ⓒ Ⓓ
29. Ⓐ Ⓑ Ⓒ Ⓓ
30. Ⓐ Ⓑ Ⓒ Ⓓ
31. Ⓐ Ⓑ Ⓒ Ⓓ
32. Ⓐ Ⓑ Ⓒ Ⓓ
33. Ⓐ Ⓑ Ⓒ Ⓓ
34. Ⓐ Ⓑ Ⓒ Ⓓ
35. Ⓐ Ⓑ Ⓒ Ⓓ
36. Ⓐ Ⓑ Ⓒ Ⓓ
37. Ⓐ Ⓑ Ⓒ Ⓓ
38. Ⓐ Ⓑ Ⓒ Ⓓ

Mathematics Achievement:
1. Ⓐ Ⓑ Ⓒ Ⓓ
2. Ⓐ Ⓑ Ⓒ Ⓓ
3. Ⓐ Ⓑ Ⓒ Ⓓ
4. Ⓐ Ⓑ Ⓒ Ⓓ
5. Ⓐ Ⓑ Ⓒ Ⓓ
6. Ⓐ Ⓑ Ⓒ Ⓓ
7. Ⓐ Ⓑ Ⓒ Ⓓ
8. Ⓐ Ⓑ Ⓒ Ⓓ
9. Ⓐ Ⓑ Ⓒ Ⓓ
10. Ⓐ Ⓑ Ⓒ Ⓓ
11. Ⓐ Ⓑ Ⓒ Ⓓ
12. Ⓐ Ⓑ Ⓒ Ⓓ
13. Ⓐ Ⓑ Ⓒ Ⓓ
14. Ⓐ Ⓑ Ⓒ Ⓓ
15. Ⓐ Ⓑ Ⓒ Ⓓ
16. Ⓐ Ⓑ Ⓒ Ⓓ
17. Ⓐ Ⓑ Ⓒ Ⓓ
18. Ⓐ Ⓑ Ⓒ Ⓓ
19. Ⓐ Ⓑ Ⓒ Ⓓ
20. Ⓐ Ⓑ Ⓒ Ⓓ
21. Ⓐ Ⓑ Ⓒ Ⓓ
22. Ⓐ Ⓑ Ⓒ Ⓓ
23. Ⓐ Ⓑ Ⓒ Ⓓ
24. Ⓐ Ⓑ Ⓒ Ⓓ
25. Ⓐ Ⓑ Ⓒ Ⓓ
26. Ⓐ Ⓑ Ⓒ Ⓓ
27. Ⓐ Ⓑ Ⓒ Ⓓ
28. Ⓐ Ⓑ Ⓒ Ⓓ
29. Ⓐ Ⓑ Ⓒ Ⓓ
30. Ⓐ Ⓑ Ⓒ Ⓓ

ISEE Lower Level Practice Test 3

Quantitative Reasoning

38 questions

Total time for this test: 35 Minutes

You may NOT use a calculator for this test.

1) Which of the following is greater than $\frac{12}{8}$?
A. $\frac{1}{2}$
B. $\frac{5}{2}$
C. $\frac{3}{4}$
D. 1

2) If $\frac{1}{2}$ of a number is greater than 8, the number must be .....
A. Less than 4
B. Equal to 8
C. Equal to 16
D. Greater than 16

3) If $4 \times (M + N) = 20$ and M is greater than 0, then N could Not be .....
A. 1
B. 2
C. 3
D. 5

4) Which of the following is closest to 5.03?
A. 6
B. 5.5
C. 5
D. 5.4

5) At a Zoo, the ratio of lions to tigers is 10 to 6. Which of the following could NOT be the total number of lions and tigers in the zoo?
A. 64
B. 80
C. 98
D. 104

6) In the multiplication bellow, A represents which digit?
$$14 \times 3A2 = 4,788$$
A. 2
B. 3
C. 4
D. 6

7) If N is an even number, which of the following is always an odd number?
A. $\frac{N}{2}$
B. $N + 4$
C. $2N$
D. $N + 1$

8) $8.9 - 4.08$ is closest to which of the following.
A. 4.1
B. 4.8
C. 6
D. 8

$$x = 2,456 \qquad y = 259$$

9) Numbers x and y are shown above. How many times larger is the value of digit 5 in the number x, than the value of digit 5 in the number y?
A. 1
B. 10
C. 100
D. 1,000

10) If 4 added to a number, the sum is 20. If the same number added to 25, the answer is
A. 30
B. 35
C. 41
D. 45

11) $\frac{3+4+8\times1+1}{4+2} = ?$
A. $\frac{15}{8}$
B. $\frac{4}{8}$
C. $\frac{8}{3}$
D. $\frac{6}{8}$

12) What is the Area of the square shown in the following square?
A. 2
B. 4
C. 6
D. 8

13) If 20 is the product of 4 and x, then 20 can be divided by which of the following?
A. $x + 4$
B. $2x - 4$
C. $x - 2$
D. $x \times 4$

14) Use the equations below to answer the question:
$$x + 13 = 19$$
$$17 + y = 22$$
What is the value of $x + y$?

A. 9
B. 10
C. 11
D. 12

15) Which of the following expressions has the same value as $\frac{5}{4} \times \frac{6}{2}$?

A. $\frac{6 \times 3}{4}$
B. $\frac{6 \times 2}{4}$
C. $\frac{5 \times 6}{4}$
D. $\frac{5 \times 3}{4}$

16) When 4 is added to three times number N, the result is 40. Then N is ….
A. 11
B. 12
C. 14
D. 16

17) At noon, the temperature was 15 degrees. By midnight, it had dropped another 20 degrees. What was the temperature at midnight?
A. 10 *degrees above zero*
B. 10 *degrees below zero*
C. 5 *degrees above zero*
D. 5 *degrees below zero*

18) If a triangle has a base of 5 cm and a height of 8 cm, what is the area of the triangle?
A. 15 cm^2
B. 20 cm^2
C. 40 cm^2
D. 45 cm^2

19) Which formula would you use to find the area of a square?
A. $length \times width \times height$
B. $\frac{1}{2} base \times height$
C. $length \times width$
D. $side \times side$

20) What is the next number in this sequence?   2, 5, 9, 14, 20, ...
A. 27
B. 26
C. 25
D. 21

21) What is the average of the following numbers?   9, 10, 12, 23, 46
A. 19
B. 20
C. 22
D. 24

22) If there are 8 red balls and 12 blue balls in a basket, what is the probability that John will pick out a red ball from the basket?
A. $\frac{18}{10}$
B. $\frac{2}{5}$
C. $\frac{2}{10}$
D. $\frac{3}{5}$

23) How many lines of symmetry does an equilateral triangle have?
A. 5
B. 4
C. 3
D. 2

24) What is 5% of 200?
A. 5
B. 10
C. 20
D. 40

25) Which of the following statement is False?
A. $2 \times 2 = 4$
B. $(4 + 1) \times 5 = 25$
C. $6 \div (3 - 1) = 1$
D. $6 \times (4 - 2) = 12$

26) If all the sides in the following figure are of equal length and length of one side is 4, what is the perimeter of the figure?
A. 15
B. 18
C. 20
D. 24

27) $\frac{4}{5} - \frac{3}{5} = ?$
A. 0.3
B. 0.25
C. 0.2
D. 0.15

28) If $N = 2$ and $\frac{32}{N} + 4 = \square$, then $\square$ = ...
A. 30
B. 32
C. 24
D. 20

29) Four people can paint 4 houses in 10 days. How many people are needed to paint 8 houses in 5 days?
A. 6
B. 8
C. 12
D. 16

30) What is the median of these numbers? 4, 9, 14, 8, 15, 18, 5
A. 8
B. 9
C. 13
D. 15

The result of a research shows the number of men and women in four cities of a country.

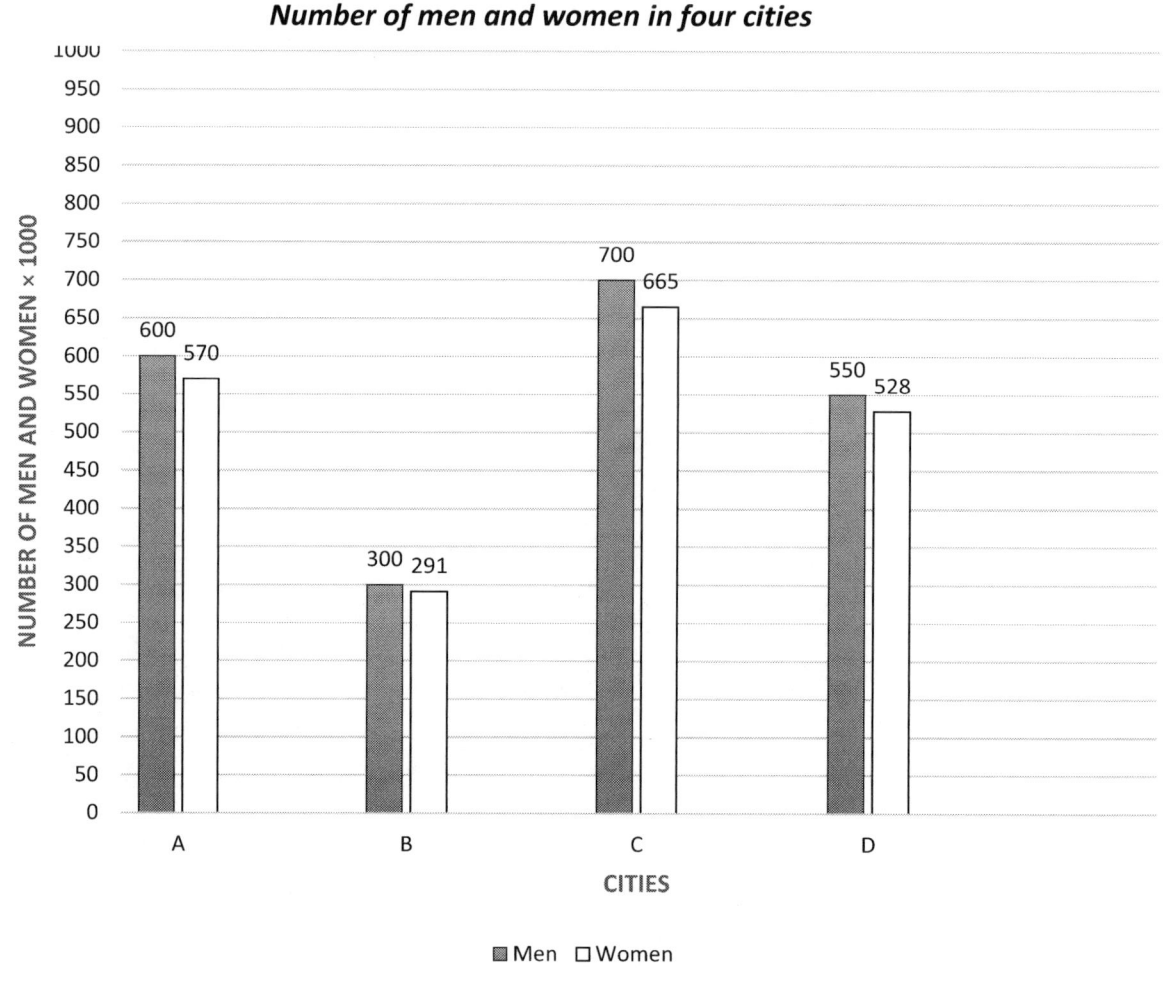

31) What is the difference of the population of women between the biggest city and smallest city?
A. 200
B. 300
C. 374
D. 409

32) What is 5,231.49245 rounded to the nearest tenth?
A. 5,231.492
B. 5,231.5
C. 5,231
D. 5,231.49

33) $19a + 22 = 41, a = ?$
A. 1
B. 4
C. 11
D. 12

34) Two angles of a triangle measure 35 and 75. What is the measure of third angle?
A. 50
B. 60
C. 65
D. 70

35) A woman weighs 135 pounds. She gains 16 pounds one month and 8 pounds the next month. What is her new weight?
A. 152 Pounds
B. 146 Pounds
C. 159 Pounds
D. 138 Pounds

36) In a basket, there are equal numbers of red, white, yellow, blue and purple cards. Which of the following could be the number of cards in the basket?
A. 121
B. 82
C. 68
D. 55

37) Jim types 72 words per minute. How many words does he type in 15 seconds?
A. 15
B. 18
C. 22
D. 25

38) Which of the following is NOT equal to $\frac{3}{7}$?
A. $\frac{33}{77}$
B. $\frac{12}{28}$
C. $\frac{27}{63}$
D. $\frac{14}{48}$

IF YOU FINISH BEFORE TIME IS CALLED, YOU MAY CHECK YOUR WORK ON THIS SECTION ONLY. DO NOT TURN TO ANY OTHER SECTION IN THE TEST. **STOP**

ISEE Lower Level Practice Test 3

Mathematics Achievement

30 questions

Total time for this test: 30 Minutes

You may NOT use a calculator for this test.

1) What's the next number in the series $\{20, 17, 14, 11, ?\}$
A. 8
B. 12
C. 6
D. 15

2) What's the least common multiple (LCM) of 8 and 14?
A. 8 and 14 have no common multiples
B. 112
C. 96
D. 56

3) Which of the following is NOT a factor of 50?
A. 5
B. 2
C. 10
D. 15

4) While at work, Emma checks her email once every 90 minutes. In 9-hour, how many times does she check her email?
A. 9 Times
B. 8 Times
C. 7 Times
D. 6 Times

5) ___ $+18 - 6 = 50$ what is the missing number?
A. 38
B. 42
C. 46
D. 52

6) Which of the following fractions is the largest?
A. $\frac{3}{4}$
B. $\frac{2}{5}$
C. $\frac{7}{9}$
D. $\frac{2}{3}$

7) A bag contains 18 balls: two green, five black, eight blue, a brown, a red and one white. If 17 balls are removed from the bag at random, what is the probability that a brown ball has been removed?

A. $\frac{1}{9}$
B. $\frac{1}{6}$
C. $\frac{16}{17}$
D. $\frac{17}{18}$

8) From last year, the price of gasoline has increased from $1.25 per gallon to $1.75 per gallon. The new price is what percent of the original price?
A. 72%
B. 120%
C. 140%
D. 160%

9) Emma purchased a computer for $450. The computer is regularly priced at $600. What was the percent discount Emma received on the computer?
A. 12%
B. 20%
C. 25%
D. 30%

10) In the given diagram, the height is 9 cm. what is the area of the triangle?

A. 23 cm^2
B. 46 cm^2
C. 126 cm^2
D. 252 cm^2

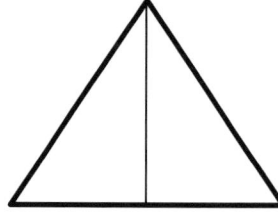

28 cm

11) Two angles of a triangle measure 51 and 47. What is the measure of the third angle?
A. 82
B. 99
C. 102
D. 262

12) If a rectangular swimming pool has a perimeter of 120 feet and is 24 feet wide, what is its area?
   A. 1,496
   B. 1,190
   C. 946
   D. 864

13) Mike is 7.5 miles ahead of Julia running at 5.5 miles per hour and Julia is running at the speed of 6 miles per hour. How long does it take Julia to catch Mike?
   A. 2 $hours$
   B. 5.5 $hours$
   C. 7.5 $hours$
   D. 15 $hours$

14) Julie gives 8 pieces of candy to each of her friends. If Julie gives all her candy away, which amount of candy could have been the amount she distributed?
   A. 187
   B. 216
   C. 243
   D. 223

15) A taxi driver earns $9 per 1-hour work. If he works 10 hours a day and in 1 hour he uses 2-liters petrol with price $1 for 1-liter. How much money does he earn in one day?
   A. $90
   B. $88
   C. $70
   D. $60

16) Convert 0.025 to a percent.
   A. 0.03%
   B. 0.25%
   C. 2.50%
   D. 25%

17) The number 0.04 can also represented by which of the following?
   A. $\frac{4}{10}$
   B. $\frac{4}{100}$
   C. $\frac{4}{1,000}$
   D. $\frac{4}{10,000}$

18) The width of a box is one third of its length. The height of the box is one third of its width. If the length of the box is 27 cm, what is the volume of the box?

A. $81\ cm^3$
B. $162 cm^3$
C. $243\ cm^3$
D. $729\ cm^3$

19) 125 students took an exam and 25 of them failed. What percent of the students passed the exam?

A. 20%
B. 40%
C. 60%
D. 80%

20) $\dfrac{\begin{array}{r}37\text{ hr. }25\text{ min.}\\ 23\text{ hr. }38\text{ min.}\end{array}}{}$

A. $12\ hr.\ 57\ min.$
B. $12\ hr.\ 47\ min.$
C. $13\ hr.\ 47\ min.$
D. $13\ hr.\ 57\ min.$

21) Which of the following is an obtuse angle?

A. 116°
B. 80°
C. 68°
D. 25°

Use the following table to answer question below.

DANIEL'S BIRD-WATCHING PROJECT	
DAY	NUMBER OF RAPTORS SEEN
Monday	?
Tuesday	10
Wednesday	15
Thursday	13
Friday	6
MEAN	10

22) This table shows the data Daniel collects while watching birds for one week. How many raptors did Daniel see on Monday?

A. 6
B. 11
C. 12
D. 13

23) In the following figure, the shaded squares are what fractional part of the whole set of squares?

A. $\frac{1}{2}$
B. $\frac{5}{8}$
C. $\frac{2}{3}$
D. $\frac{3}{5}$

24) If a box contains red and blue balls in ratio of 3 : 2 red to blue, how many red balls are there if 90 blue balls are in the box?

A. 140
B. 135
C. 80
D. 30

25) A shirt costing $200 is discounted 25%. After a month, the shirt is discounted another 15%. Which of the following expressions can be used to find the selling price of the shirt?
A. $(200)(0.70)$
B. $(200) - 200(0.30)$
C. $(200)(0.15) - (200)(0.15)$
D. $(200)(0.75)(0.85)$

26) Emma draws a shape on her paper. The shape has four sides. It has only one pair of parallel sides. What shape does Emma draw?
A. parallelogram
B. rectangle
C. square
D. trapezoid

27) If $A = 20$, then which of the following equations are correct?
A. $A + 20 = 40$
B. $A \div 20 = 40$
C. $20 \times A = 40$
D. $A - 20 = 40$

28) Joe makes $3.75 per hour at his work. If he works 8 hours, how much money will he earn?
A. $22.00
B. $24.75
C. $26.50
D. $30.00

29) In a classroom of 54 students, 18 are male. About what percentage of the class is female?

A. 43%
B. 55%
C. 67%
D. 79%

30) Nancy ordered 19 pizzas. Each pizza has 8 slices. How many slices of pizza did Nancy ordered?
A. 124
B. 152
C. 156
D. 180

IF YOU FINISH BEFORE TIME IS CALLED, YOU MAY CHECK YOUR WORK ON THIS SECTION ONLY. DO NOT TURN TO ANY OTHER SECTION IN THE TEST. **STOP**

ISEE LOWER Level Math Practice Test 4

2019 - 2020

Two Parts

Total number of questions: 68

Quantitative Reasoning: 38 questions

Mathematics Achievement: 30 questions

Total time for two parts: 65 Minutes

ISEE Lower Level Practice Test Answer Sheets

Remove (or photocopy) these answer sheets and use them to complete the practice tests.

ISEE Lower Level Practice Test 4

Quantitative Reasoning

#		#	
1	Ⓐ Ⓑ Ⓒ Ⓓ	21	Ⓐ Ⓑ Ⓒ Ⓓ
2	Ⓐ Ⓑ Ⓒ Ⓓ	22	Ⓐ Ⓑ Ⓒ Ⓓ
3	Ⓐ Ⓑ Ⓒ Ⓓ	23	Ⓐ Ⓑ Ⓒ Ⓓ
4	Ⓐ Ⓑ Ⓒ Ⓓ	24	Ⓐ Ⓑ Ⓒ Ⓓ
5	Ⓐ Ⓑ Ⓒ Ⓓ	25	Ⓐ Ⓑ Ⓒ Ⓓ
6	Ⓐ Ⓑ Ⓒ Ⓓ	26	Ⓐ Ⓑ Ⓒ Ⓓ
7	Ⓐ Ⓑ Ⓒ Ⓓ	27	Ⓐ Ⓑ Ⓒ Ⓓ
8	Ⓐ Ⓑ Ⓒ Ⓓ	28	Ⓐ Ⓑ Ⓒ Ⓓ
9	Ⓐ Ⓑ Ⓒ Ⓓ	29	Ⓐ Ⓑ Ⓒ Ⓓ
10	Ⓐ Ⓑ Ⓒ Ⓓ	30	Ⓐ Ⓑ Ⓒ Ⓓ
11	Ⓐ Ⓑ Ⓒ Ⓓ	31	Ⓐ Ⓑ Ⓒ Ⓓ
12	Ⓐ Ⓑ Ⓒ Ⓓ	32	Ⓐ Ⓑ Ⓒ Ⓓ
13	Ⓐ Ⓑ Ⓒ Ⓓ	33	Ⓐ Ⓑ Ⓒ Ⓓ
14	Ⓐ Ⓑ Ⓒ Ⓓ	34	Ⓐ Ⓑ Ⓒ Ⓓ
15	Ⓐ Ⓑ Ⓒ Ⓓ	35	Ⓐ Ⓑ Ⓒ Ⓓ
16	Ⓐ Ⓑ Ⓒ Ⓓ	36	Ⓐ Ⓑ Ⓒ Ⓓ
17	Ⓐ Ⓑ Ⓒ Ⓓ	37	Ⓐ Ⓑ Ⓒ Ⓓ
18	Ⓐ Ⓑ Ⓒ Ⓓ	38	Ⓐ Ⓑ Ⓒ Ⓓ
19	Ⓐ Ⓑ Ⓒ Ⓓ		
20	Ⓐ Ⓑ Ⓒ Ⓓ		

Mathematics Achievement

#		#	
1	Ⓐ Ⓑ Ⓒ Ⓓ	21	Ⓐ Ⓑ Ⓒ Ⓓ
2	Ⓐ Ⓑ Ⓒ Ⓓ	22	Ⓐ Ⓑ Ⓒ Ⓓ
3	Ⓐ Ⓑ Ⓒ Ⓓ	23	Ⓐ Ⓑ Ⓒ Ⓓ
4	Ⓐ Ⓑ Ⓒ Ⓓ	24	Ⓐ Ⓑ Ⓒ Ⓓ
5	Ⓐ Ⓑ Ⓒ Ⓓ	25	Ⓐ Ⓑ Ⓒ Ⓓ
6	Ⓐ Ⓑ Ⓒ Ⓓ	26	Ⓐ Ⓑ Ⓒ Ⓓ
7	Ⓐ Ⓑ Ⓒ Ⓓ	27	Ⓐ Ⓑ Ⓒ Ⓓ
8	Ⓐ Ⓑ Ⓒ Ⓓ	28	Ⓐ Ⓑ Ⓒ Ⓓ
9	Ⓐ Ⓑ Ⓒ Ⓓ	29	Ⓐ Ⓑ Ⓒ Ⓓ
10	Ⓐ Ⓑ Ⓒ Ⓓ	30	Ⓐ Ⓑ Ⓒ Ⓓ
11	Ⓐ Ⓑ Ⓒ Ⓓ		
12	Ⓐ Ⓑ Ⓒ Ⓓ		
13	Ⓐ Ⓑ Ⓒ Ⓓ		
14	Ⓐ Ⓑ Ⓒ Ⓓ		
15	Ⓐ Ⓑ Ⓒ Ⓓ		
16	Ⓐ Ⓑ Ⓒ Ⓓ		
17	Ⓐ Ⓑ Ⓒ Ⓓ		
18	Ⓐ Ⓑ Ⓒ Ⓓ		
19	Ⓐ Ⓑ Ⓒ Ⓓ		
20	Ⓐ Ⓑ Ⓒ Ⓓ		

ISEE Lower Level Practice Test 4

Quantitative Reasoning

38 questions

Total time for this test: 35 Minutes

You may NOT use a calculator for this test

1) $\frac{8}{2} - \frac{3}{2} = ?$
A. 1
B. 1.5
C. 2
D. 2.5

2) If $48 = 3 \times N + 12$, then $N = ...$
A. 8
B. 12
C. 14
D. 15

3) When 7 is added to four times a number N, the result is 23. Which of the following equations represents this statement?
A. $4 + 7N = 23$
B. $23N + 4 = 7$
C. $4N + 7 = 23$
D. $4N + 23 = 7$

4) When 78 is divided by 5, the remainder is the same as when 45 is divided by
A. 2
B. 4
C. 5
D. 7

5) John has 3,400 cards and Max has 606 cards. How many more cards does John have than Max?
A. 2,794
B. 1,798
C. 1,812
D. 1,828

6) In the following right triangle, what is the value of x?
A. 15
B. 30
C. 45
D. 60

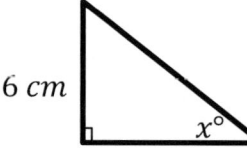

7) What is 4 percent of 480?
A. 16
B. 19.2
C. 30
D. 40

8) In a basket, the ratio of red marbles to blue marbles is 3 to 2. Which of the following could NOT be the total number of red and blue marbles in the basket?
A. 15
B. 32
C. 55
D. 60

9) A square has an area of $81 cm^2$. What is its perimeter?
A. $28\ cm^2$
B. $32\ cm^2$
C. $34\ cm^2$
D. $36\ cm^2$

10) Find the missing number in the sequence: $5, 8, 12, \ldots, 23$
A. 15
B. 17
C. 18
D. 20

11) The length of a rectangle is 3 times of its width. If the length is 18, what is the perimeter of the rectangle?
A. 24
B. 30
C. 36
D. 48

12) Mary has y dollars. John has $9 more than Mary. If John gives Mary $12, then in terms of y, how much does John have now?
A. $y + 1$
B. $y + 10$
C. $y - 3$
D. $y - 1$

13) Dividing 107 by 6 leaves a remainder of
A. 1
B. 2
C. 3
D. 5

14) If $4,000 + A - 200 = 7,400$, then $A =$
A. 200
B. 1600
C. 3,600
D. 4,200

15) For what price is 15 percent off the same as $75 off?
A. $200
B. $300
C. $350
D. $500

16) Which of the following fractions is less than $\frac{3}{2}$?
A. 1.4
B. $\frac{5}{2}$
C. 3
D. 2.8

17) Use the equation below to answer the question.
$$x + 5 = 6$$
$$2y = 8$$
What is the value of $y - x$?

A. 3
B. 4
C. 5
D. 6

18) If $310 - x + 114 = 225$, then $x = $?
A. 101
B. 156
C. 199
D. 211

19) Of the following, 25 percent of $43.99 is closest to
A. $9.90
B. $10.00
C. $11.00
D. $11.50

20) Solve.
$$8.08 - 5.6 = \ ....$$
A. 2.42
B. 2.46
C. 2.48
D. 3

21) If $500 + \square - 180 = 1,100$, then $\square = ?$
A. 580
B. 660
C. 700
D. 780

22) There are 60 students in a class. If the ratio of the number of girls to the total number of students in the class is $\frac{1}{6}$, which are the following is the number of boys in that class?
A. 10
B. 20
C. 25
D. 50

23) If $N \times (5 - 3) = 12$ then $N = ?$
A. 6
B. 12
C. 13
D. 14

24) If $x \blacksquare y = 3x + y - 2$, what is the value of $4 \blacksquare 12$?
A. 4
B. 18
C. 22
D. 36

25) Of the following, which number if the greatest?
A. 0.092
B. 0.8913
C. 0.8923
D. 0.8896

26) $\frac{7}{8} - \frac{3}{4} = ?$
A. 0.125
B. 0.375
C. 0.5
D. 0.625

27) Which of the following is the closest to 4.02?
A. 4
B. 4.2
C. 4.3
D. 4.5

28) Which of the following statements is False?
A. $(7 \times 2 + 14) \times 2 = 56$
B. $(2 \times 5 + 4) \div 2 = 7$
C. $3 + (3 \times 8) = 27$
D. $14 \div (2 + 5) = 5$

29) A trash container, when empty, weighs 45 pounds. If this container is filled with a load of trash that weighs 240 pounds, what is the total weight of the container and its contents?
A. 224 *pounds*
B. 285 *pounds*
C. 295 *pounds*
D. 325 *pounds*

30) During the six-month period shown, what is the median number of shirts per month?
A. 130
B. 140
C. 145
D. 147.5

31) A writer finishes 180 pages of his manuscript in 20 hours. How many pages is his average?
A. 18
B. 16
C. 12
D. 9

32) The distance between cities A and B is approximately 2,600 miles. If you drive an average of 68 miles per hour, how many hours will it take you to drive from city A to city B?
A. *approximately* 41 *hours*
B. *approximately* 38 *hours*
C. *approximately* 29 *hours*
D. *approximately* 27 *hours*

33) $\frac{13}{25}$ is equal to:
A. 5.2
B. 0.052
C. 0.52
D. 0.5

34) $12a + 20 = 140, a = ?$
A. 8
B. 10
C. 14
D. 18

35) What is the place value of 2 in 5.7325?
A. hundredths
B. thousandths
C. ten thousandths
D. hundred thousandths

36) Which of the following is NOT a prime factor of 90?
A. 2
B. 3
C. 5
D. 9

37) Which of these numbers is equal to $\frac{85}{1,000}$?
A. 8.5
B. 0.85
C. 0.085
D. 0.0085

38) During a 26-hour day, Moe works $\frac{1}{2}$ of the time. How many hours does Moe work in that day?
A. 18
B. 16
C. 14
D. 13

IF YOU FINISH BEFORE TIME IS CALLED, YOU MAY CHECK YOUR WORK ON THIS SECTION ONLY. DO NOT TURN TO ANY OTHER SECTION IN THE TEST. **STOP**

ISEE Lower Level Practice Test 4

Mathematics Achievement

30 questions

Total time for this test: 30 Minutes

You may NOT use a calculator for this test.

1) What's the next number in the series {29, 24, 19, 14, ?}
   A. 14
   B. 9
   C. 4
   D. 1

2) What's the greatest common factor of the 18 and 32?
   A. 11
   B. 12
   C. 2
   D. 4

3) Which of the following is NOT a multiple of 5?
   A. 12
   B. 30
   C. 15
   D. 20

4) A right triangle has sides with lengths 6, 8 and 10. What is the perimeter of the triangle?
   A. 480
   B. 36
   C. 24
   D. 18

5) What is the name of a rectangle with sides of equal length?
   A. Hexagon
   B. Octagon
   C. Pentagon
   D. Square

6) With what number must 5.685321 be multiplied in order to obtain the number 56,853.21?
   A. 100
   B. 1,000
   C. 10,000
   D. 100,000

7) Which expression is equal to $\frac{3}{11}$?
   1) $3 - 11$
   2) $3 \div 11$
   3) 3×11
   4) $\frac{11}{3}$

8) Lily and Ella are in a pancake–eating contest. Lily can eat three pancakes per minute, while Ella can eat $2\frac{1}{4}$ pancakes per minute. How many total pancakes can they eat in 5 minutes?

A. 30.5 Pancakes
B. 29.5 Pancakes
C. 26.25 Pancakes
D. 11.5 Pancakes

9) Which expression has a value of −8?
A. $8 - (-2) + (-18)$
B. $2 + (-3) \times (-2)$
C. $-6 \times (-6) + (-2) \times (-12)$
D. $(-2) \times (-7) + 4$

10) What is the sum of $0.87 + 1.4 + 3.23 = ?$
A. 3.2
B. 2.5
C. 5.5
D. 14.63

11) What is the perimeter of a rectangle that has a length of 8 inches and a width of 5 inches?
A. 13
B. 23
C. 26
D. 28

12) How many $\frac{1}{4}$ cup servings are in a package of cheese that contains $6\frac{1}{2}$ cups altogether?
A. 20
B. 22
C. 24
D. 26

13) If this clock shows a time in the morning, what time was it 6 hours and 30 minutes ago?

A. 07:45 AM
B. 05:45 AM
C. 07:45 PM
D. 05:45 PM

14) The area of a rectangle is 72 square meters. The width is 8 meters. What is the length of the rectangle?
A. 8
B. 9
C. 10
D. 12

Use the table below to answer the question.

City Populations

City	Population
Denton	28,097
Bomberg	29,207
Windham	30,700
Sanhill	25,980

15) Which list of city populations is in order from least to greatest?

A. 28,097; 29,207; 30,700; 25,980

B. 30,700; 29,207; 28,097; 25,980

C. 25,980; 28,097; 29,207; 30,700

D. 25,980; 29,207; 28,097; 30,700

16) The temperature on Sunday at 12:00 PM was 76°F. Low temperature on the same day was 24°F cooler. Which temperature is closest to the low temperature on that day?
A. 76°F
B. 52°F
C. 51°F
D. 75°

17) $(5 + 7) \div (3^2 \div 2) =$ ___
A. 12
B. $\frac{15}{7}$
C. 5
D. 4

18) Ella buys five items costing $2.26, $14.69, $2.50, $4.66, and $17.99. What is the estimated total cost of Ella's items?
A. between $25 and $30
B. between $30 and $35
C. between $35 and $40
D. between $40 and $45

19) How long is the line segment shown on the number line below?
A. 6
B. 7
C. 8
D. 9

20) There are 86 students from Riddle Elementary school at the library on Monday. The other 32 students in the school are practicing in the classroom. Which number sentence shows the total number of students in Riddle Elementary school?
A. $86 + 32$
B. $86 - 32$
C. 86×32
D. $86 \div 32$

21) $\frac{11}{19}$ is equal to:
A. 0.579
B. 5.79
C. 57.90
D. 579.00

22) Which number correctly completes the number sentence $80 \times 34 = ?$
A. 272
B. 560
C. 1,920
D. 2,720

23) What fraction of each shape is shaded?

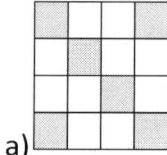 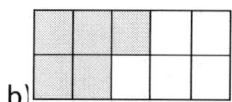
a) b)

A. a. $\frac{5}{16}$; b. $\frac{5}{10}$
B. a. $\frac{6}{16}$; b. $\frac{5}{16}$
C. a. $\frac{6}{16}$; b. $\frac{5}{10}$
D. a. $\frac{8}{16}$; b. $\frac{4}{10}$

24) Which statement about the number 945,382.16 is true?

A. The digit 6 has a value of (6×100)
B. The digit 4 has a value of (4×100)
C. The digit 8 has a value of (8×10)
D. The digit 5 has a value of (5×100)

25) Ella described a number using these clues:
Three – digit odd numbers that have a 5 in the hundreds place and a 2 in the tens place

Which number could fit Ella's description?
A. 517
B. 527
C. 522
D. 526

26) The following graph shows the mark of six students in mathematics. What is the mean (average) of the marks?

A. 15
B. 14.5
C. 14
D. 13.5

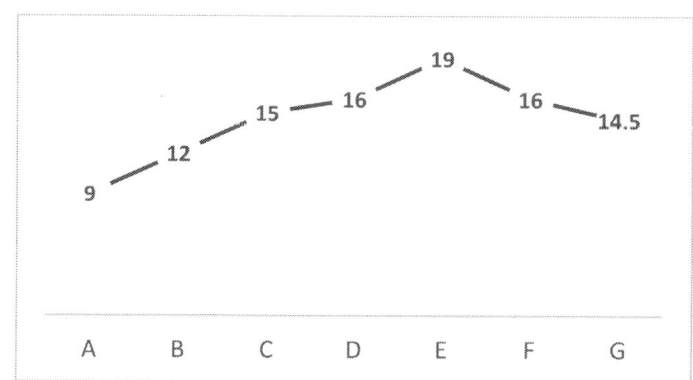

27) In the deck of cards, there are 4 spades, 3 hearts, 7 clubs, and 10 diamonds. What is the probability that William will pick out a spade?

A. $\frac{1}{6}$
B. $\frac{1}{8}$
C. $\frac{1}{9}$
D. $\frac{1}{5}$

28) Jason's favorite sports team has won 0.62 of its games this season. How can Jason express this decimal as a fraction?

A. $\frac{6}{2}$
B. $\frac{62}{10}$
C. $\frac{6.2}{100}$
D. $\frac{62}{100}$

29) Which fraction has the least value?

A. $\frac{1}{2}$
B. $\frac{3}{8}$
C. $\frac{3}{4}$
D. $\frac{9}{16}$

30) There are 365 days in a year, and 24 hours in a day. How many hours are in a year?

A. 2,190
B. 7,440
C. 7,679
D. 8,760

ISEE LOWER Level Math Practice Test 5

2019 - 2020

Two Parts

Total number of questions: 68

Quantitative Reasoning: 38 questions

Mathematics Achievement: 30 questions

Total time for two parts: 65 Minutes

ISEE Lower Level Practice Test Answer Sheets

Remove (or photocopy) these answer sheets and use them to complete the practice tests.

ISEE Lower Level Practice Test 5

Quantitative Reasoning

#		#	
1	Ⓐ Ⓑ Ⓒ Ⓓ	21	Ⓐ Ⓑ Ⓒ Ⓓ
2	Ⓐ Ⓑ Ⓒ Ⓓ	22	Ⓐ Ⓑ Ⓒ Ⓓ
3	Ⓐ Ⓑ Ⓒ Ⓓ	23	Ⓐ Ⓑ Ⓒ Ⓓ
4	Ⓐ Ⓑ Ⓒ Ⓓ	24	Ⓐ Ⓑ Ⓒ Ⓓ
5	Ⓐ Ⓑ Ⓒ Ⓓ	25	Ⓐ Ⓑ Ⓒ Ⓓ
6	Ⓐ Ⓑ Ⓒ Ⓓ	26	Ⓐ Ⓑ Ⓒ Ⓓ
7	Ⓐ Ⓑ Ⓒ Ⓓ	27	Ⓐ Ⓑ Ⓒ Ⓓ
8	Ⓐ Ⓑ Ⓒ Ⓓ	28	Ⓐ Ⓑ Ⓒ Ⓓ
9	Ⓐ Ⓑ Ⓒ Ⓓ	29	Ⓐ Ⓑ Ⓒ Ⓓ
10	Ⓐ Ⓑ Ⓒ Ⓓ	30	Ⓐ Ⓑ Ⓒ Ⓓ
11	Ⓐ Ⓑ Ⓒ Ⓓ	31	Ⓐ Ⓑ Ⓒ Ⓓ
12	Ⓐ Ⓑ Ⓒ Ⓓ	32	Ⓐ Ⓑ Ⓒ Ⓓ
13	Ⓐ Ⓑ Ⓒ Ⓓ	33	Ⓐ Ⓑ Ⓒ Ⓓ
14	Ⓐ Ⓑ Ⓒ Ⓓ	34	Ⓐ Ⓑ Ⓒ Ⓓ
15	Ⓐ Ⓑ Ⓒ Ⓓ	35	Ⓐ Ⓑ Ⓒ Ⓓ
16	Ⓐ Ⓑ Ⓒ Ⓓ	36	Ⓐ Ⓑ Ⓒ Ⓓ
17	Ⓐ Ⓑ Ⓒ Ⓓ	37	Ⓐ Ⓑ Ⓒ Ⓓ
18	Ⓐ Ⓑ Ⓒ Ⓓ	38	Ⓐ Ⓑ Ⓒ Ⓓ
19	Ⓐ Ⓑ Ⓒ Ⓓ		
20	Ⓐ Ⓑ Ⓒ Ⓓ		

Mathematics Achievement

#		#	
1	Ⓐ Ⓑ Ⓒ Ⓓ	21	Ⓐ Ⓑ Ⓒ Ⓓ
2	Ⓐ Ⓑ Ⓒ Ⓓ	22	Ⓐ Ⓑ Ⓒ Ⓓ
3	Ⓐ Ⓑ Ⓒ Ⓓ	23	Ⓐ Ⓑ Ⓒ Ⓓ
4	Ⓐ Ⓑ Ⓒ Ⓓ	24	Ⓐ Ⓑ Ⓒ Ⓓ
5	Ⓐ Ⓑ Ⓒ Ⓓ	25	Ⓐ Ⓑ Ⓒ Ⓓ
6	Ⓐ Ⓑ Ⓒ Ⓓ	26	Ⓐ Ⓑ Ⓒ Ⓓ
7	Ⓐ Ⓑ Ⓒ Ⓓ	27	Ⓐ Ⓑ Ⓒ Ⓓ
8	Ⓐ Ⓑ Ⓒ Ⓓ	28	Ⓐ Ⓑ Ⓒ Ⓓ
9	Ⓐ Ⓑ Ⓒ Ⓓ	29	Ⓐ Ⓑ Ⓒ Ⓓ
10	Ⓐ Ⓑ Ⓒ Ⓓ	30	Ⓐ Ⓑ Ⓒ Ⓓ
11	Ⓐ Ⓑ Ⓒ Ⓓ		
12	Ⓐ Ⓑ Ⓒ Ⓓ		
13	Ⓐ Ⓑ Ⓒ Ⓓ		
14	Ⓐ Ⓑ Ⓒ Ⓓ		
15	Ⓐ Ⓑ Ⓒ Ⓓ		
16	Ⓐ Ⓑ Ⓒ Ⓓ		
17	Ⓐ Ⓑ Ⓒ Ⓓ		
18	Ⓐ Ⓑ Ⓒ Ⓓ		
19	Ⓐ Ⓑ Ⓒ Ⓓ		
20	Ⓐ Ⓑ Ⓒ Ⓓ		

ISEE Lower Level Practice Test 5

Quantitative Reasoning

38 questions

Total time for this test: 35 Minutes

You may NOT use a calculator for this test.

1) $\frac{10}{4} - \frac{3}{4} = ?$
   A. 1
   B. 1.75
   C. 2
   D. 2.25

2) If $68 = 4 \times N + 12$, then $N = ...$
   A. 10
   B. 14
   C. 24
   D. 35

3) When 5 is added to six times a number N, the result is 27. Which of the following equations represents this statement?
   A. $6 + 5N = 27$
   B. $27N + 6 = 5$
   C. $6N + 5 = 27$
   D. $6N + 27 = 5$

4) When 58 is divided by 5, the remainder is the same as when 66 is divided by
   A. 2
   B. 4
   C. 5
   D. 7

5) John has 3,600 cards and Max has 707 cards. How many more cards does John have than Max?
   A. 2,893
   B. 2,798
   C. 2,612
   D. 2,528

6) In the following right triangle, what is the value of x?
   A. 15
   B. 30
   C. 45
   D. 60

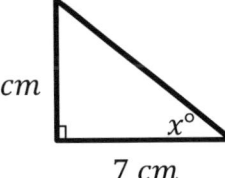

7) What is 5 percent of 580?
   A. 20
   B. 29
   C. 30
   D. 40

8) In a basket, the ratio of red marbles to blue marbles is 1 to 5. Which of the following could NOT be the total number of red and blue marbles in the basket?
A. 12
B. 26
C. 54
D. 72

9) A square has an area of $49\ cm^2$. What is its perimeter?
A. $18\ cm^2$
B. $28\ cm^2$
C. $34\ cm^2$
D. $36\ cm^2$

10) Find the missing number in the sequence: 6, 9, 13, 18, … ..
A. 20
B. 24
C. 25
D. 26

11) The length of a rectangle is 3 times of its width. If the length is 27, what is the perimeter of the rectangle?
A. 24
B. 30
C. 48
D. 72

12) Mary has y dollars. John has $11 more than Mary. If John gives Mary $14, then in terms of y, how much does John have now?
A. $y + 1$
B. $y + 11$
C. $y - 3$
D. $y - 1$

13) Dividing 108 by 5 leaves a remainder of
A. 6
B. 5
C. 4
D. 3

14) If $5{,}000 + A - 300 = 8{,}400$, then $A =$
A. 1200
B. 1600
C. 3,700
D. 4,200

15) For what price is 25 percent off the same as $90 off?
A. $280
B. $300
C. $320
D. $360

16) Which of the following fractions is less than $\frac{7}{5}$?
A. 1.2
B. $\frac{7}{2}$
C. 3
D. 3.8

17) Use the equation below to answer the question.
$$x + 4 = 6$$
$$2y = 10$$
What is the value of $y - x$?
A. 2
B. 3
C. 4
D. 5

18) If $320 - x + 116 = 235$, then $x = $?
A. 101
B. 156
C. 201
D. 221

19) Of the following, 25 percent of $63.99 is closest to
A. $9.90
B. $12.00
C. $16.00
D. $16.50

20) Solve.
$$8.08 - 4.6 = ...$$
A. 5.58
B. 4.46
C. 3.98
D. 3.48

21) If $700 + \square - 180 = 1,300$, then $\square = ?$
A. 580
B. 660
C. 700
D. 780

22) There are 65 students in a class. If the ratio of the number of girls to the total number of students in the class is $\frac{1}{5}$, which are the following is the number of boys in that class?
A. 10
B. 20
C. 25
D. 52

23) If $N \times (6 - 4) = 18$ then $N = ?$
A. 9
B. 12
C. 15
D. 18

24) If $x \blacksquare y = 4x + y - 2$, what is the value of $5 \blacksquare 20$?
A. 20
B. 28
C. 38
D. 39

25) Of the following, which number if the greatest?
A. 0.062
B. 0.6913
C. 0.6923
D. 0.6896

26) $\frac{10}{8} - \frac{3}{4} = ?$
A. 0.125
B. 0.5
C. 0.57
D. 0.625

27) Which of the following is the closest to 7.02?
A. 7
B. 7.2
C. 7.3
D. 7.5

28) Which of the following statements is False?
A. $(7 \times 2 + 14) \times 2 = 56$
B. $(2 \times 5 + 4) \div 2 = 7$
C. $3 + (3 \times 9) = 30$
D. $15 \div (2 + 3) = 4$

29) A trash container, when empty, weighs 35 pounds. If this container is filled with a load of trash that weighs 275 pounds, what is the total weight of the container and its contents?

A. $224\ pounds$
B. $310\ pounds$
C. $345\ pounds$
D. $355\ pounds$

30) Which of the following is a whole number greater than 44?
A. 4,400.50
B. 440
C. $44\frac{1}{2}$
D. 43

31) A writer finishes 186 pages of his manuscript in 31 hours. How many pages is his average?
A. 18
B. 15
C. 10
D. 6

32) The distance between cities A and B is approximately 3,500 miles. If Nicole drives an average of 50 miles per hour, how many hours will it take her to drive from city A to city B?

A. $approximately\ 79\ hours$
B. $approximately\ 70\ hours$
C. $approximately\ 49\ hours$
D. $approximately\ 27\ hours$

33) $\frac{4}{25}$ is equal to:

A. 5.2
B. 0.26
C. 0.16
D. 0.016

34) $10a + 30 = 150, a = ?$

A. 10
B. 12
C. 15
D. 18

35) What is the place value of 4 in 7.7345?

A. Hundredths
B. Thousandths
C. Ten thousandths
D. Hundred thousandths

36) Which of the following is NOT a prime factor of 60?
A. 2
B. 3
C. 5
D. 6

37) Which of these numbers is equal to $\frac{45}{1,000}$?

A. 4.5
B. 0.45
C. 0.045
D. 0.0045

38) During a 24-hour day, Moe works $\frac{1}{8}$ of the time. How many hours does Moe work in that day?

A. 8
B. 6
C. 4
D. 3

IF YOU FINISH BEFORE TIME IS CALLED, YOU MAY CHECK YOUR WORK ON THIS SECTION ONLY. DO NOT TURN TO ANY OTHER SECTION IN THE TEST. **STOP**

ISEE Lower Level Practice Test 5

Mathematics Achievement

30 questions

Total time for this test: 30 Minutes

You may NOT use a calculator for this test.

1) Which is sixty-five thousand, eight hundred nineteen?

A. 65,819
B. 650,819
C. 605,819
D. 658,019

2) What's the greatest common factor of 22 and 32?

A. 16
B. 9
C. 2
D. 1

3) Which of the following is not a multiple of 6?

A. 10
B. 30
C. 18
D. 24

4) A right triangle has sides with lengths 3, 4 and 5. What is the perimeter of the triangle?
A. 5
B. 10
C. 12
D. 25

5) What is 3,666 divided by 6?
A. 687
B. 666
C. 622
D. 611

6) With what number must 4.674321 be multiplied in order to obtain the number 46,743.21?
A. 100
B. 1,000
C. 10,000
D. 100,000

7) Which expression is equal to $\frac{7}{11}$?
A. $7 - 11$
B. $7 \div 11$
C. 7×11
D. $\frac{11}{7}$

8) Lily and Ella are in a pancake–eating contest. Lily can eat two pancakes per minute, while Ella can eat $2\frac{1}{2}$ pancakes per minute. How many total pancakes can they eat in 5 minutes?
A. 9.5 *Pancakes*
B. 29.5 *Pancakes*
C. 22.5 *Pancakes*
D. 11.5 *Pancakes*

9) Which expression has a value of 8?
A. $8- (-2) + (-18)$
B. $2 + (-3) \times (-2)$
C. $-6 \times (-6) + (-2) \times (-12)$
D. $(-2) \times (-7) + 4$

10) $0.97 + 1.6 + 4.23 = ?$

A. 6
B. 6.2
C. 6.8
D. 6.9

11) What is the perimeter of a rectangle that has a length of 6 inches and a width of 7 inches?
A. 13
B. 26
C. 28
D. 29

12) How many $\frac{1}{8}$ cup servings are in a package of cheese that contains $6\frac{1}{2}$ cups altogether?
A. 20
B. 42
C. 43
D. 52

13) If the $\frac{?}{24} = \frac{2}{3}$
A. 8
B. 12
C. 16
D. 18

14) The area of a rectangle is 63 square meters. The width is 9 meters. What is the length of the rectangle?
A. 6
B. 7
C. 9
D. 12

15) $55.09 - 12.34 =$
A. 28.70
B. 34.25
C. 42.75
D. 48.26

16) The temperature on Sunday at $12:00\ PM$ was $87°F$. Low temperature on the same day was $35°F$ cooler. Which temperature is closest to the low temperature on that day?
A. $76°F$
B. $52°F$
C. $41°F$
D. $35°$

17) $(12 + 4) \div (4^2 \div 2) =$ ___
A. $\frac{16}{4}$
B. 3
C. 2
D. 1

18) Ella buys five items costing $4.26, $16.69, $2.50, $4.66, and $17.99. What is the estimated total cost of Ella's items?
A. between $25 and $30
B. between $30 and $35
C. between $35 and $40
D. between $45 and $50

19) How long is the line segment shown on the number line below?
A. 6
B. 7
C. 8
D. 9

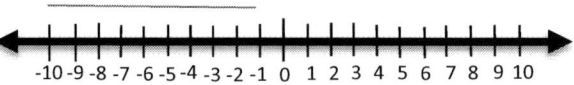

20) There are 97 students from Riddle Elementary school at the library on Monday. The other 33 students in the school are practicing in the classroom. Which number sentence shows the total number of students in Riddle Elementary school?

A. $97 + 33$
B. $97 - 33$
C. 97×33
D. $97 \div 33$

21) $\frac{13}{20}$ is equal to:

A. 0.65
B. 0.065
C. 6.5
D. 65.5

22) Which number correctly completes the number sentence $90 \times 46 = ?$

A. 372
B. 2660
C. 3,920
D. 4,140

23) ___ $+ 12 - 8 = 55$
What is the missing number?

A. 34
B. 43
C. 51
D. 55

24) Which statement about the number 749,382.15 is true?

A. *The digit 5 has a value of* (5×100)
B. *The digit 4 has a value of* (4×100)
C. *The digit 8 has a value of* (8×10)
D. *The digit 9 has a value of* (9×100)

25) Ella described a number using these clues:
Three – digit odd numbers that have a 6 in the hundreds place and a 3 in the tens place

Which number could fit Ella's description?

A. 627
B. 637
C. 632
D. 636

26) The following graph shows the mark of six students in mathematics. What is the mean (average) of the marks?

A. 15
B. 13.85
C. 12.3
D. 11.5

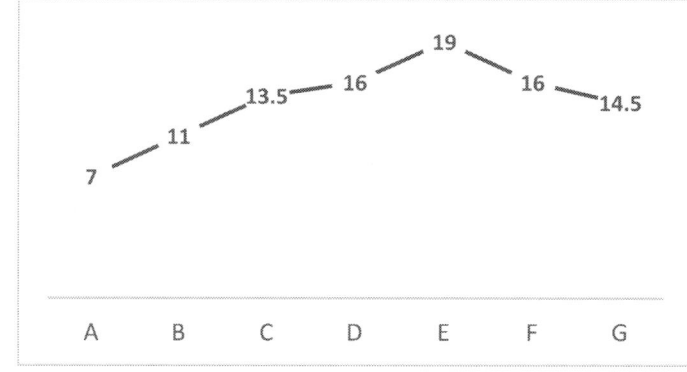

27) In the deck of cards, there are 3 spades, 4 hearts, 8 clubs, and 9 diamonds. What is the probability that William will pick out a spade?

A. $\frac{1}{6}$
B. $\frac{1}{8}$
C. $\frac{1}{9}$
D. $\frac{1}{5}$

28) Jason's favorite sports team has won 0.92 of its games this season. How can Jason express this decimal as a fraction?

A. $\frac{9}{2}$
B. $\frac{92}{10}$
C. $\frac{92}{100}$
D. $\frac{9.2}{10}$

29) Which fraction has the least value?

A. $\frac{5}{6}$
B. $\frac{3}{8}$
C. $\frac{3}{4}$
D. $\frac{15}{16}$

30) The width of a box is 4 ft, its length is 5 ft, and its height is 3 ft. What is the volume of the box?
A. 12 cubic feet
B. 23 cubic feet
C. 48 cubic feet
D. 60 cubic feet

IF YOU FINISH BEFORE TIME IS CALLED, YOU MAY CHECK YOUR WORK ON THIS SECTION ONLY. DO NOT TURN TO ANY OTHER SECTION IN THE TEST. **STOP**

ISEE Lower Level Math Practice Tests Answers and Explanations

ISEE Lower Level Math Practice Test 1 Answer Key									
Quantitative Reasoning						Mathematics Achievement			
1	B	17	D	33	A	1	D	17	B
2	D	18	B	34	D	2	D	18	D
3	D	19	B	35	C	3	D	19	D
4	C	20	A	36	D	4	D	20	C
5	C	21	B	37	C	5	A	21	A
6	C	22	B	38	D	6	C	22	A
7	D	23	C			7	D	23	D
8	B	24	B			8	C	24	B
9	A	25	C			9	B	25	D
10	C	26	D			10	C	26	D
11	C	27	C			11	A	27	A
12	D	28	D			12	D	28	D
13	B	29	D			13	D	29	C
14	C	30	B			14	A	30	B
15	D	31	C			15	C		
16	B	32	B			16	C		

ISEE Lower Level Math Practice Test 2 Answer Key

Quantitative Reasoning | Mathematics Achievement

#	Ans	#	Ans	#	Ans		#	Ans	#	Ans
1	D	17	B	33	C		1	A	17	C
2	B	18	C	34	B		2	C	18	D
3	C	19	C	35	B		3	A	19	D
4	D	20	C	36	D		4	C	20	A
5	A	21	D	37	C		5	D	21	A
6	C	22	D	38	D		6	C	22	D
7	B	23	A				7	B	23	C
8	B	24	C				8	C	24	C
9	B	25	C				9	D	25	B
10	B	26	B				10	C	26	B
11	D	27	A				11	B	27	A
12	C	28	D				12	D	28	C
13	D	29	B				13	C	29	B
14	C	30	B				14	B	30	D
15	D	31	D				15	C		
16	A	32	B				16	B		

ISEE Lower Level Math Practice Test 3 Answer Key

Quantitative Reasoning						Mathematics Achievement			
1	B	16	B	31	C	1	A	16	C
2	D	17	D	32	B	2	D	17	B
3	D	18	B	33	A	3	D	18	D
4	C	19	D	34	D	4	D	19	D
5	C	20	A	35	C	5	A	20	C
6	C	21	B	36	D	6	C	21	A
7	D	22	B	37	B	7	D	22	A
8	B	23	C	38	D	8	C	23	D
9	A	24	B			9	B	24	B
10	C	25	C			10	C	25	D
11	C	26	D			11	A	26	D
12	B	27	C			12	D	27	A
13	D	28	D			13	D	28	D
14	C	29	D			14	B	29	C
15	D	30	B			15	C	30	B

ISEE Lower Level Math Practice Test 4 Answer Key

Quantitative Reasoning						Mathematics Achievement			
1	D	16	A	31	D	1	B	16	B
2	B	17	A	32	B	2	B	17	D
3	C	18	C	33	C	3	A	18	D
4	D	19	C	34	B	4	C	19	D
5	A	20	C	35	B	5	D	20	A
6	C	21	D	36	D	6	C	21	A
7	B	22	D	37	C	7	B	22	D
8	B	23	A	38	D	8	C	23	C
9	D	24	C			9	A	24	C
10	B	25	C			10	C	25	B
11	D	26	A			11	C	26	B
12	C	27	A			12	D	27	A
13	D	28	D			13	C	28	D
14	C	29	B			14	B	29	B
15	D	30	D			15	C	30	D

ISEE Lower Level Math Practice Test 5 Answer Key

Quantitative Reasoning | Mathematics Achievement

#	Ans	#	Ans	#	Ans		#	Ans	#	Ans
1	B	17	B	33	C		1	A	17	C
2	B	18	C	34	B		2	C	18	D
3	C	19	C	35	B		3	A	19	D
4	D	20	D	36	D		4	C	20	A
5	A	21	D	37	C		5	D	21	A
6	C	22	D	38	D		6	C	22	D
7	B	23	A				7	B	23	C
8	B	24	C				8	C	24	C
9	B	25	C				9	B	25	B
10	B	26	B				10	C	26	B
11	D	27	A				11	B	27	B
12	C	28	D				12	D	28	C
13	D	29	B				13	C	29	B
14	C	30	B				14	B	30	D
15	D	31	D				15	C		
16	A	32	B				16	B		

Score Your Test

ISEE scores are broken down by four sections: Verbal Reasoning, Reading Comprehension, Quantitative Reasoning, and Mathematics Achievement. A sum of the ALL sections is also reported. The Essay section is scored separately.

For the Lower Level ISEE, the score range is 760 to 940, the lowest possible score a student can earn is 760 and the highest score is 940 for each section. A student receives 1 point for every correct answer. There is no penalty for wrong or skipped questions.

The total scaled score for a Lower Level ISEE test is the sum of the scores for all sections. A student will also receive a percentile score of between 1-99% that compares that student's test scores with those of other test takers of same grade and gender from the past 3 years. When a student receives her/his score, the percentile score is also be broken down into a stanine and the stanines are ranging from 1–9. Most schools accept students with scores of 5–9. The ideal candidate has scores of 6 or higher.

Percentile Rank	Stanine
1 – 3	1
4 – 10	2
11- 22	3
23 - 39	4
40 – 59	5
60 – 76	6
77- 88	7
89 – 95	8
96 - 99	9

The following charts provide an estimate of students ISEE percentile rankings for the practice tests, compared against other students taking these tests. Keep in mind that these percentiles are estimates only, and your actual ISEE percentile will depend on the specific group of students taking the exam in your year.

ISEE Lower Level Quantitative Reasoning Percentiles			
Grade Applying to	**25th Percentile**	**50th Percentile**	**75th Percentile**
Grade 5	825	840	860
Grade 6	838	855	870

ISEE Lower Level Mathematics Achievement Percentiles			
Grade Applying to	**25th Percentile**	**50th Percentile**	**75th Percentile**
Grade 5	830	850	865
Grade 6	855	865	978

Use the next table to convert ISEE Lower level raw score to scaled score for application to grade 5 and grade 6.

ISEE Lower Level Scaled Scores

Raw Score	Quantitative Reasoning		Mathematics Achievement		Raw Score	Quantitative Reasoning		Mathematics Achievement	
	Grade 5	Grade 6	Grade 5	Grade 6		Grade 5	Grade 6	Grade 5	Grade 6
0	760	760	760	760	26	900	885	900	890
1	770	765	770	765	27	905	890	910	900
2	780	770	780	770	28	910	895	925	920
3	790	775	790	775	29	910	900	935	930
4	800	780	800	780	30	915	905	940	940
5	810	785	810	785	31	920	910		
6	820	790	820	790	32	925	915		
7	825	795	825	795	33	930	920		
8	830	800	830	800	34	930	925		
9	835	805	835	805	35	930	925		
10	840	810	840	810	36	935	930		
11	845	815	845	815	37	935	935		
12	850	820	850	820	38	940	940		
13	855	825	855	825					
14	860	830	855	830					
15	865	835	860	835					
16	870	840	860	840					
17	875	845	865	840					
18	880	845	865	845					
19	880	850	870	845					
20	885	855	870	850					
21	885	860	875	850					
22	890	865	875	855					
23	890	870	875	855					
24	895	875	880	860					
25	895	880	890	880					

# ISEE Lower Level Test 1 Practice Tests
Quantitative Reasoning

1) **Choice B is correct.**

    $\frac{14}{8} = \frac{7}{4} = 1.75$, the only choice that is greater than 1.75 is $\frac{5}{2}$. (Recall that $\frac{4}{3} = 1.33..$), $\frac{5}{2} = 2.5$, $2.5 > 1.75$

2) **Choice D is correct.**

    If $\frac{1}{3}$ of a number is greater than 9, the number must be greater than 27. $\frac{1}{3}x > 9$ →multiply both sides of the inequality by 3, then: $x > 27$

3) **Choice D is correct.**

    $5 \times (M + N) = 25$, then $M + N = 5$. $M > 0 \rightarrow N$ could not be 5

4) **Choice C is correct.**

    The closest to 4.03 is 4 in the choices provided.

5) **Choice C is correct.**

    The ratio of lions to tigers is 12 to 4 or 3 to 1 at the zoo. Therefore, total number of lions and tigers must be divisible by 4. $3 + 1 = 4$, From the numbers provided, only 98 is not divisible by 4.

6) **Choice C is correct.**

    A represents digit 4 in the multiplication. $12 \times 342 = 4,104$

7) **Choice D is correct.**

    M is even. Let's choose 2 and 4 for M. Now, let's review the choices provided.

    A) $\frac{M}{2} = \frac{2}{2} = 1, \quad \frac{M}{2} = \frac{4}{2} = 2,$ One result is odd and the other one is even.
    B) $M + 4 = 2 + 4 = 6, 4 + 4 = 8$ Both results are even.
    C) $4M = 4 \times 2 = 8, 4 \times 4 = 16$ Both results are even.
    D) $M + 3 = 2 + 3 = 5, 4 + 3 = 7$ Both results are odd.

8) **Choice B is correct.**

    $9.9 - 5.08 = 4.82$, which is closest to 4.8

9) **Choice A is correct.**

    The value of digit 2 in both numbers x and y are in the tens place. Therefore, they have the same value.

10) **Choice C is correct.**

Let x be the number. Then: $5 + x = 20 \rightarrow x = 15 \rightarrow 15 + 35 = 50$

11) **Choice C is correct.**

$$\frac{2 + 5 + 6 \times 1 + 1}{6 + 2} = \frac{14}{8} = \frac{7}{4}$$

12) **Choice D is correct.**

$7 \times 4 \times 12 \times 3$ is equal to the product of 28 and 36. $(7 \times 4) \times (12 \times 3) = 28 \times 36$

13) **Choice B is correct.**

$20 = x \times 5 \rightarrow x = 20 \div 5 = 4$, x equals to 4. Let's review the choices provided:
A) $x + 4 \rightarrow 4 + 4 = 8$ 20 is not divisible by 8.
B) $2x - 4 \rightarrow 2 \times 4 - 4 = 4$ 20 is divisible by 4.
C) $x - 1 \rightarrow 4 - 1 = 3$ 20 is not divisible by 3.
D) $x \times 4 \rightarrow 4 \times 4 = 16$ 20 is not divisible by 16.

The answer is B.

14) **Choice C is correct.**

$x + 12 = 18 \rightarrow x = 6, 17 + y = 21 \rightarrow y = 4, x + y = 6 + 4 = 10$

15) **Choice D is correct.**

$\frac{2}{5} \times \frac{10}{4} = \frac{20}{20} = 1$, Choice D is equal to: $\frac{5 \times 4}{20} = \frac{20}{20} = 1$

16) **Choice B is correct.**

$5 + 3N = 50 \rightarrow 3N = 50 - 5 = 45 \rightarrow N = 15$

17) **Choice D is correct.**

$15 - 25 = -10$, The temperature at midnight was 10 degrees below zero.

18) **Choice B is correct.**

Area of a triangle = $\frac{1}{2} \times (base) \times (height) = \frac{1}{2} \times 6 \times 9 = 27$

19) **Choice B is correct.**

$area\ of\ a\ triangle = \frac{1}{2} \times (base) \times (height)$

20) **Choice A is correct.**

First, find the pattern, $3 + 3 = 6 \rightarrow 6 + 4 = 10 \rightarrow 10 + 5 = 15 \rightarrow 15 + 6 = 21$
The difference of two consecutive numbers increase by 1. The difference of 15 and 21 is 6.
So, the next number should be 28. $21 + 7 = 28$

21) **Choice B is correct.**

$$average = \frac{sum\ of\ all\ numbers}{number\ of\ numbers} = \frac{7 + 11 + 12 + 23 + 45}{5} = 19.6$$

22) Choice B is correct.

There are 8 red ball and 24 are total number of balls. Therefore, probability that John will pick out a red ball from the basket is 8 out of 24 or $\frac{8}{8+16} = \frac{8}{24} = \frac{1}{3}$.

23) Choice C is correct.

The perimeter of a square is 4 times one side. The perimeter of the square is 24, then its side is 6. $24 \div 4 = 6$

24) Choice B is correct.

$$10\ percent\ of\ 300 = 10\%\ of\ 300 = \frac{10}{100} \times 300 = 30$$

25) Choice C is correct.

Let's review the options provided:
A) $3 \times 3 = 9$ This is true!
B) $(4 + 1) \times 5 = 25$ This is true!
C) $6 \div (4 - 1) = 1 \rightarrow 6 \div 3 = 2$ This is NOT true!
D) $6 \times (4 - 2) = 12 \rightarrow 6 \times 2 = 12$ This is true!

26) Choice D is correct.

The shape has 6 equal sides. And is side is 5. Then, the perimeter of the shape is: $5 \times 6 = 30$

27) Choice C is correct.

$$\frac{4}{5} - \frac{2}{5} = \frac{2}{5} = 0.4$$

28) Choice D is correct.

$N = 2$, then: $\frac{64}{2} + 8 = 32 + 8 = 40$

29) Choice D is correct.

From choices provided only $\frac{8}{21}$ is not equal to $\frac{1}{3}$. $\frac{8}{21} \neq \frac{1}{3}$

30) Choice B is correct.

Write the numbers in order: $3, 5, 8, 10, 13, 15, 19$, Median is the number in the middle. Therefore, the median is 10.

31) Choice C is correct.

The biggest city is city C and the smallest city is city B. Number of men in city A is 700 and number of men in city C is 300. Then: $700 - 300 = 400$

32) Choice B is correct

4,231.48245 rounded to the nearest tenth is 4,231.5

33) Choice A is correct

$18a + 32 = 50$, $18a = 50 - 32$, $18a = 18$, $a = 1$

34) Choice D is correct

All angles in a triangle sum up to 180 degrees. Two angles of a triangle measure 30 and 65.

$30 + 65 = 95$, Then, the third angle is: $180 - 95 = 85$

35) Choice C is correct

$145 + 15 + 9 = 169$

36) Choice D is correct

There are equal numbers of four types of cards. Therefore, the total number of cards must be divisible by 4. Only choice D (56) is divisible by 4.

37) Choice C is correct

15 seconds is one fourth of a minute. One fourth of 88 is 22. $88 \div 4 = 22$. Jim types 22 words in 15 seconds.

38) Choice D is correct

From the choice provided, only choice D is not equal to $\frac{2}{7}$. $\frac{12}{48} = \frac{1}{4}$

ISEE Lower Level Practice Test 1

Mathematics Achievement

1) Choice D is correct

Find common denominator and solve. $\frac{1}{5} + \frac{3}{4} = \frac{4}{20} + \frac{15}{20} = \frac{19}{20}$

2) Choice D is correct

least common multiple (LCM) of 6 and 16 is the smallest number that is divisible by both 6 and 16. $LCM = 48$

3) **Choice D is correct**

   The factors of 45 are: { 1, 3, 5, 9, 15, 45}. 12 is not a factor of 45.

4) **Choice D is correct**

   8 $hour = 480$ minutes. Write a proportion and solve. $\frac{80}{1} = \frac{480}{x}$ → $x = \frac{480}{80} = 6$

5) **Choice A is correct**

   2,923.2769 rounded to the nearest tenth is 2,923.3

6) **Choice C is correct**

   One method to compare fractions is to convert them to decimals.

   A. $\frac{3}{4} = 0.75$, B. $\frac{1}{5} = 0.2$, C. $\frac{8}{9} = 0.88$, D. $\frac{2}{3} = 0.66$, 0.88 or $\frac{8}{9}$ is the largest number.

7) **Choice D is correct**

   If 17 balls are removed from the bag at random, there will be one ball in the bag. The probability of choosing a brown ball is 1 out of 18. Therefore, the probability of not choosing a brown ball is 17 out of 18 and the probability of having not a brown ball after removing 17 balls is the same.

8) **Choice C is correct**

   $$\frac{1.75}{1.40} = 1.25 = 125\%$$

9) **Choice B is correct**

   $$\frac{504}{600} = 0.84 = 84\%$$

   504 is 84% of 600. Therefore, the discount is: $100\% - 84\% = 16\%$

10) **Choice C is correct**

    $Area\ of\ a\ triangle = \frac{1}{2}(base)(height)$, $A = \frac{1}{2}(26)(6) = 78$

11) **Choice A is correct**

    All angles in a triangle add up to 180 degrees. $50 + 45 = 95$, $180 - 95 = 85$

12) **Choice D is correct**

$Perimeter = 2(width + length)$, $A = width \times length$, First, find the length of the rectangle. $Perimeter = 2(width + length) \to 112 = 2(22 + length) \to 112 = 44 + 2(length) \to 68 = 2(length) \to length = 34$, $A = 22 \times 34 = 748$

13) Choice D is correct.

Since Julia running at 6.5 miles per hour and she is running at the speed of 7 miles per hour, each hour their distance decreases by 0.5 mile. So, it takes 17 hours to cover distance of 8.5 miles. $8.5 \div 0.5 = 17$

14) Choice A is correct

Since Julie gives 6 pieces of candy to each of her friends, then, then number of pieces of candies must be divisible by 6.

A. $180 \div 6 = 30$
B. $217 \div 6 = 36.16$
C. $243 \div 6 = 40.5$
D. $263 \div 6 = 43.83$

Only choice A gives a whole number.

15) Choice C is correct

$\$8 \times 10 = \$80$, Petrol use: $10 \times 2 = 20$ liters, Petrol cost: $20 \times \$1 = \$20$

Money earned: $\$80 - \$20 = \$60$

16) Choice C is correct

$0.035 \times 100 = 3.5\%$

17) Choice B is correct

$\frac{3}{100} = 0.03$

18) Choice D is correct

If the length of the box is 24, then the width of the box is one third of it, 8, and the height of the box is 4 (half the width). The volume of the box is:

$V = (length)(width)(height) = (24)(8)(4) = 768 m^3$

19) Choice D is correct.

The failing rate is 20 out of 125 $= \frac{20}{125}$, Change the fraction to percent: $\frac{20}{125} \times 100\% = 16\%$

16 percent of students failed. Therefore, 84 percent of students passed the exam.

20) Choice C is correct

```
25 hr. 25 min.
− 23 hr. 38 min.
  1 hr. 47 min.
```

21) Choice A is correct

An obtuse angle is an angle of greater than 90 degrees and less than 180 degrees. Only choice A is an obtuse angle.

22) Choice A is correct

Let x be the number of raptors Daniel saw on Monday. Then:

$Mean = \frac{x+9+14+12+5}{5} = 20 \rightarrow x + 40 = 100 \rightarrow x = 100 - 40 = 60$

23) Choice D is correct.

There are 15 squares and 8 of them are shaded. Therefore, 8 out of 15 or $\frac{8}{15}$ are shaded.

24) Choice B is correct

Write a proportion and solve. $\frac{2}{3} = \frac{x}{60}$, Use cross multiplication: $3x = 120 \rightarrow x = 40$

25) Choice D is correct

To find the discount, multiply the number by $(100\% - rate\ of\ discount)$.

Therefore, for the first discount we get: $(700)(100\% - 15\%) = (700)(0.85)$

For the next 15% discount: $(700)(0.85)(0.85)$

26) Choice D is correct.

A square has four equal sides and angles.

27) Choice A is correct.

Plug in 30 for A in the equation. Only choice A works. $A + 20 = 50$, $30 + 20 = 50$

28) Choice D is correct

$1\ hour: \$4.75$, $7\ hours: 7 \times \$4.75 = \$33.25$

29) Choice C is correct.

There are 44 students in the class. 20 of the are male and 24 of them are female.

24 out of 44 are female. Then: $\frac{24}{44} = \frac{x}{100} \rightarrow 2,400 = 44x \rightarrow x = 2,400 \div 44 \approx 55\%$

30) Choice B is correct.

1 pizza has 8 slices. 17 pizzas contain $(17 \times 8) 136$ slices.

ISEE Lower Level Practice Test 2
Quantitative Reasoning

1) **Choice D is correct.**
   $$\frac{10}{2} - \frac{3}{2} = \frac{7}{2} = 3.5$$

2) **Choice B is correct.**
   $58 = 2 \times N + 12 \rightarrow 2N = 58 - 12 = 46 \rightarrow N = 23$

3) **Choice C is correct.**
   Four times a number N is $4 \times N$. When 3 is added to it, the result is: $3 + (4 \times N) = 24 \rightarrow 4N + 3 = 24$

4) **Choice D is correct.**
   105 divided by 6, the remainder is 3. 87 divided by 4, the remainder is also 3.

5) **Choice A is correct.**

   $2,400 - 506 = 1,894$

6) **Choice C is correct.**

   All angles in a triangle sum up to 180 degrees. The triangle provided is an isosceles triangle. In an isosceles triangle, the three angles are 45, 45, and 90 degrees. Therefore, the value of x is 45.

7) **Choice B is correct.**
   $$5 \; percent \; of \; 360 = \frac{5}{100} \times 360 = \frac{1}{20} \times 360 = \frac{360}{20} = 18$$

8) **Choice B is correct.**
   The ratio of red marbles to blue marbles is 5 to 1. Therefore, the total number of marbles must be divisible by 6. $5 + 1 = 6$, 26 is the only one that is not divisible by 6.

9) **Choice B is correct.**
   $Area \; of \; a \; square \; = \; side \times side = 64 \rightarrow side = 8$
   $Perimeter \; of \; a \; square \; = \; 4 \times side \; = \; 4 \times 8 = 32$

10) **Choice B is correct.**
    $6 + 3 = 9, \quad 9 + 4 = 13, \; 13 + 5 = 18 \; , \; 18 + 6 = 24$

11) **Choice D is correct.**
    The length of the rectangle is 24. Then, its width is 8. $24 \div 3 = 8$

    $Perimeter \; of \; a \; rectangle = 2 \times width + 2 \times length = 2 \times 8 + 2 \times 24 = 16 + 48 = 64$

12) Choice C is correct.

$Mary's\ Money = M, John's\ Money = M + 10, John\ gives\ Mary\ \$13 \to M + 10 - 13 = M - 3$

13) Choice D is correct.

Dividing 215 by 6 leaves a remainder of 5. $215 \div 6 = 35\ r5$

14) Choice C is correct.

$6,000 + A - 400 = 8,400 \to 6,000 + A = 8,400 + 400 = 8,800 \to A = 8,800 - 6,000 = 2,800$

15) Choice D is correct.

$90 off is the same as 12 percent off. Thus, 12 percent of a number is 90.

Then: $12\%\ of\ x = 90 \to 0.12x = 90 \to x = \frac{90}{0.12} = 750$

16) Choice A is correct.

$\frac{5}{2} = 2.5$, the only choice provided that is less than 2.4 is choice A. $\frac{5}{2} = 2.5 > 2.4$

17) Choice B is correct.
$x + 4 = 7 \to x = 3, 2y = 10 \to y = 5, y - x = 5 - 3 = 2$

18) Choice C is correct.
$320 - x + 216 = 425 \to 320 - x = 425 - 216 = 209 \to x = 320 - 209 = 111$

19) Choice C is correct.

25 percent of $54.00 is $13.5. (Remember that 25 percent is equal to one fourth)

20) Choice C is correct.

$9.08 - 5.6 = 3.48$

21) Choice D is correct.

$600 + \square - 180 = 1,200 \to 600 + \square = 1,200 + 180 = 1,380, \square = 1,380 - 600 = 780$

22) Choice D is correct.

$\frac{1}{5}$ of students are girls. Therefore, $\frac{4}{5}$ of students in the class are boys. $\frac{4}{5}$ of 60 is 48. There are 48 boys in the class. $\frac{4}{5} \times 60 = \frac{240}{5} = 48$

23) Choice A is correct.
$N \times (6 - 4) = 14 \to N \times 2 = 14 \to N = 7$

24) Choice C is correct.
If $x \blacksquare y = 4x + y - 2$, Then: $4 \blacksquare 16 = 4(4) + 16 - 2 = 16 + 16 - 2 = 30$

25) Choice C is correct.
Of the numbers provided, 0.9923 is the greatest.

26) Choice B is correct.

$$\frac{9}{8} - \frac{3}{4} = \frac{9}{8} - \frac{6}{8} = \frac{3}{8} = 0.375$$

27) Choice A is correct.

The closest number to 5.02 is 5.

28) Choice D is correct.

$14 \div (4 + 3) = 14 \div 7 = 2$ is not 3

29) Choice B is correct

$250 + 38 = 288$

30) Choice B is correct

Let's order number of shoes sold per month: 20, 25, 25, 35, 35, 40

Median is the number in the middle. Since, there are 6 numbers (an even number) the Median is the average of numbers 3 and 4: Median is: $\frac{25+35}{2} = 30$

31) Choice D is correct

$270 \div 30 = 9$

32) Choice B is correct

$Speed = \frac{distance}{time}, 50 = \frac{3,400}{time} \rightarrow me = \frac{3,400}{50} = 68$, It takes Nicole about 68 hours to go from city A to city B.

33) Choice C is correct

$\frac{14}{35} = 0.4$

34) Choice B is correct

$10a + 30 = 140, 10a = 140 - 30, 10a = 110, a = 11$

35) Choice B is correct

Thousandths

36) Choice D is correct

9 is NOT a prime factor. (it is divisible by 3)

37) Choice C is correct

$\frac{25}{1,000} = 0.025$

38) Choice D is correct

$\frac{1}{3}$ of 18 hours is 6 hours. $\frac{1}{3} \times 18 = \frac{18}{3} = 6$

ISEE Lower Level Practice Test 2
Mathematics Achievement

1) **Choice A is correct**

    Seventy-four thousand, eight hundred nineteen is written as 74,819.

2) **Choice C is correct**

    $$300 + 950 = 1,250$$

3) **Choice A is correct**

    From choices provided, only 12 is NOT a multiple of 7.

4) **Choice C is correct**

    The perimeter of the triangle is: $5 + 12 + 13 = 30$

5) **Choice D is correct**

    The product of 11 and 5 is 55.

6) **Choice C is correct.**

    The question is that number 66,743.12 is how many times of number 6.674312. The answer is 10,000.

7) **Choice B is correct.**

    $\frac{4}{13}$ means 4 is divided by 13. The fraction line simply means division or $\div$. Therefore, we can write $\frac{4}{13}$ as $4 \div 13$.

8) **Choice C is correct.**

    Lily eats 2 pancakes in 1 minute $\Rightarrow$ Lily eats 2×5 pancakes in 5 minutes.

    Ella eats $3\frac{1}{2}$ pancakes in 1 minute $\Rightarrow$ Ella eats $3\frac{1}{2} \times 5$ pancakes in 5 minutes.

    In total Lily and Ella eat $10 + 17.5 = 27.5$ pancakes in 5 minutes.

9) **Choice D is correct.**

    Simplify each choice provided using order of operations rules.

A. $8-(-2)+(-18) = 8+2-18 = -8$
B. $2+(-3)\times(-2) = 2+6 = 8$
C. $-6\times(-6)+(-2)\times(-12) = 36+24 = 60$
D. $(-2)\times(-7)+4 = 14+4 = 18$

Only choice D is 18.

10) Choice C is correct

$0.79 + 1.5 + 3.23 = 5.52$

11) Choice B is correct

$Perimeter\ of\ a\ rectangle = 2(length + width) = 2(6+4) = 20$

12) Choice D is correct

To solve this problem, divide $5\frac{1}{2}$ by $\frac{1}{6}$. $5\frac{1}{2} \div \frac{1}{6} = \frac{11}{2} \div \frac{1}{6} = \frac{11}{2} \times \frac{6}{1} = 33$

13) Choice C is correct.

The clock shows the time 2:15 AM. Four hours before that is 10:15 PM. And 30 minutes before that is 9:45 PM.

14) Choice B is correct.

$Area = width \times height,\ Area = 54,\ Width = 6,\ 54 = 6 \times height,\ height = \frac{54}{6} = 9$

15) Choice C is correct.

$26,980 \leq 28,097 \leq 28,307 \leq 29,900$

16) Choice B is correct.

Low temperature is 25°F cooler than the temperature at 12:00 PM that is 77°F, that means low temperature is 52°F (77°F − 25°F).

17) Choice C is correct

$(9+6) \div (3^2 \div 3) = (15) \div (9 \div 3) = (15) \div (3) = 5$

18) Choice D is correct

$3.26 + 15.69 + 2.50 + 4.66 + 17.99 = 44.1$

19) Choice D is correct

The line is from 4 to −5. $4 - (-5) = 4 + 5 = 9$

20) Choice A is correct.

To find total number of students in Riddle Elementary school, add number of all students.

$87 + 43 = 130$

21) Choice A is correct.

$\frac{12}{20} = 0.6$

22) Choice D is correct.

$70 \times 36 = 2,520$

23) Choice C is correct.

The first picture is divided to 16 parts that 6 parts of it is shaded ($\frac{6}{16}$). The second picture is divided to 10 parts that 5 parts of that is shaded ($\frac{5}{10}$).

$8 + a = 14$, then a is 6. $4 + b = 12$, then b is 8. $a + b = 6 + 8 = 14$

24) Choice C is correct.

The digit 6 has a value of $6 \times \frac{1}{100}$, The digit 4 has a value of $4 \times 10,000$, The digit 8 has a value of $8 \times 10 = 800$, The digit 5 has a value of $9 \times 1,000$. Only choice C is correct.

25) Choice B is correct.

Three – digit odd numbers that have a 7 in the hundreds place and a 3 in the tens place are $741, 743, 745, 747, 749.$ 747 is one of the choices.

26) Choice B is correct

$average\ (mean) = \frac{sum\ of\ terms}{number\ of\ terms} = \frac{8+13+15.5+16+19+16+14.5}{7} = 14.57$

27) Choice A is correct

$probability = \frac{desired\ outcomes}{possible\ outcomes} = \frac{4}{4 + 3 + 8 + 9} = \frac{4}{24} = \frac{1}{6}$

28) Choice C is correct.

0.52 is equal to $\frac{52}{100}$

29) Choice B is correct.

From fractions provided, choice B ($\frac{3}{10}$) has the least value.

30) Choice D is correct.

The closest number to 200.22 is 200.3.

ISEE Lower Level Test 3 Practice Tests
Quantitative Reasoning

1) **Choice B is correct.**

   $\frac{12}{8} = 1.5$, the only choice that is greater than 1.5 is $\frac{5}{2}$. $\frac{5}{2} = 2.5$, $2.5 > 1.5$

2) **Choice D is correct.**

   If $\frac{1}{2}$ of a number is greater than 8, the number must be greater than 16. $\frac{1}{2}x > 8$ →multiply both sides of the inequality by 2, then: $x > 16$

3) **Choice D is correct.**

   $4 \times (M + N) = 20$, then $M + N = 5$. $M > 0 \rightarrow N$ could not be 5

4) **Choice C is correct.**
   The closest to 5.03 is 5 in the options provided.

5) **Choice C is correct.**

   The ratio of lions to tigers is 10 to 6 or 5 to 3 at the zoo. Therefore, total number of lions and tigers must be divisible by 8. $5 + 3 = 8$, From the numbers provided, only 98 is not divisible by 8.

6) **Choice C is correct.**
   A represents digit 4 in the multiplication. $14 \times 342 = 4,788$

7) **Choice D is correct.**

   N is even. Let's choose 2 and 4 for N. Now, let's review the options provided.

   A) $\frac{N}{2} = \frac{2}{2} = 1$, $\frac{N}{2} = \frac{4}{2} = 2$, One result is odd and the other one is even.
   B) $N + 4 = 2 + 4 = 6$, $4 + 4 = 8$ Both results are even.
   C) $2N = 2 \times 2 = 4$, $4 \times 2 = 8$ Both results are even.
   D) $N + 1 = 2 + 1 = 3$, $4 + 1 = 5$ Both results are odd.

8) **Choice B is correct.**

$8.9 - 4.08 = 4.82$, which is closest to 4.8

9) **Choice A is correct.**

   The value of digit 5 in both numbers x and y are in the tens place. Therefore, they have the same value.

10) **Choice C is correct.**

    $4 + x = 20 \rightarrow x = 16 \rightarrow 16 + 25 = 41$

11) **Choice C is correct.**

    $$\frac{3 + 4 + 8 \times 1 + 1}{4 + 2} = \frac{16}{6} = \frac{8}{3}$$

12) **Choice B is correct.**

    $Area\ of\ a\ square\ = (one\ side) \times (one\ side) = 2 \times 2 = 4$

13) **Choice D is correct.**

    $20 = x \times 4 \rightarrow x = 20 \div 4 = 5$, x equals to 5. Let's review the options provided:
    A) $x + 4 \rightarrow 5 + 4 = 9$ 20 is not divisible by 9.
    B) $2x - 4 \rightarrow 2 \times 5 - 4 = 6$ 20 is not divisible by 6.
    C) $x - 2 \rightarrow 5 - 2 = 3$ 20 is not divisible by 3.
    D) $x \times 4 \rightarrow 5 \times 4 = 20$ 20 is divisible by 20.

    The answer is D.

14) **Choice C is correct.**

    $x + 13 = 19 \rightarrow x = 6, 17 + y = 22 \rightarrow y = 5, x + y = 6 + 5 = 11$

15) **Choice D is correct.**

    $\frac{5}{4} \times \frac{6}{2} = \frac{30}{8} = \frac{15}{4}$, Choice D is equal to $\frac{15}{4}$. $\frac{5 \times 3}{4} = \frac{15}{4}$

16) **Choice B is correct.**

    $4 + 3N = 40 \rightarrow 3N = 40 - 4 = 36 \rightarrow N = 12$

17) **Choice D is correct.**

    $15 - 20 = -5$, The temperature at midnight was 5 degrees below zero.

18) **Choice B is correct.**

    $Area\ of\ a\ triangle\ = \frac{1}{2} \times (base) \times (height) = \frac{1}{2} \times 5 \times 8 = 20$

19) **Choice D is correct.**

    $Area\ of\ a\ squre\ =\ side \times side$

20) **Choice A is correct.**

$2 + 3 = 5 \rightarrow 5 + 4 = 9 \rightarrow 9 + 5 = 14 \rightarrow 14 + 6 = 20 \rightarrow 20 + 7 = 27$

21) **Choice B is correct.**

$$average = \frac{sum\ of\ all\ numbers}{number\ of\ numbers} = \frac{9 + 10 + 12 + 23 + 46}{5} = 20$$

22) **Choice B is correct.**

There are 8 red ball and 20 are total number of balls. Therefore, probability that John will pick out a red ball from the basket is 8 out of 20 or $\frac{8}{8+12} = \frac{8}{20} = \frac{2}{5}$.

23) **Choice C is correct.**

An equilateral triangle has 3 lines of symmetry.

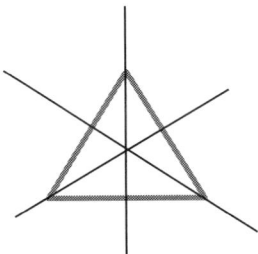

24) **Choice B is correct.**

$$5 \text{ percent of } 200 = 5\% \text{ of } 200 = \frac{5}{100} \times 200 = 10$$

25) **Choice C is correct.**

Let's review the options provided:

A) $2 \times 2 = 4$ This is true!
B) $(4 + 1) \times 5 = 25$ This is true!
C) $6 \div (3 - 1) = 1 \rightarrow 6 \div 2 = 3$ This is NOT true!
D) $6 \times (4 - 2) = 12 \rightarrow 6 \times 2 = 12$ This is true!

26) **Choice D is correct.**

The shape has 6 equal sides. And is side is 4. Then, the perimeter of the shape is: $4 \times 6 = 24$

27) **Choice C is correct.**

$\frac{4}{5} - \frac{3}{5} = \frac{1}{5} = 0.2$

28) **Choice D is correct.**

$N = 2$, then: $\frac{32}{2} + 4 = 16 + 4 = 20$

29) **Choice D is correct.**

Four people can paint 4 houses in 10 days. It means that for painting 8 houses in 10 days we need 8 people. To paint 8 houses in 5 days, 16 people are needed.

30) Choice B is correct.

Write the numbers in order: 4, 5, 8, 9, 14, 15, 18, Median is the number in the middle. Therefore, the median is 9.

31) Choice C is correct.

The population of women in city C is 665 and in city B is 291. Then: $665 - 291 = 374$

32) Choice B is correct

5,231.49245 rounded to the nearest tenth is 5231.5

33) Choice A is correct

$19a + 22 = 41, 19a = 41 - 22, 19a = 19, a = 1$

34) Choice D is correct

$35 + 75 = 110, 180 - 110 = 70$

35) Choice C is correct

$135 + 16 + 8 = 159$

36) Choice D is correct

There are equal numbers of five types of cards. Therefore, the total number of cards must be divisible by 5. Only choice D (55) is divisible by 5.

37) Choice B is correct

15 seconds is one fourth of a minute. One fourth of 72 is 18. $72 \div 4 = 18$. Jim types 18 words in 15 seconds.

38) Choice D is correct

From the choice provided, only choice D is not equal to $\frac{3}{7}$. $\frac{14}{48} = \frac{7}{24}$

ISEE Lower Level Practice Test 3 Explanations
MATHEMATICS ACHIVEMENT

1) **Choice A is correct**

   $\{20, 17, 14, 11, 8\}$

2) **Choice D is correct**

   $LCM = 56$

3) **Choice D is correct**

   The factors of 50 are: $\{1, 2, 5, 10, 25, 50\}$

4) **Choice D is correct**

   $9\ hour = 540\ minutes,\ \frac{90}{1} = \frac{540}{x}\ \rightarrow\ x = \frac{540}{90} = 6$

5) **Choice A is correct**

   ___ $+ 18 - 6 = 50$. The missing number is 38.

6) **Choice C is correct**

   a. $\frac{3}{4} = 0.75$, b. $\frac{2}{5} = 0.4$, c. $\frac{7}{9} = 0.77$, d. $\frac{2}{3} = 0.66$

7) **Choice D is correct**

   If 17 balls are removed from the bag at random, there will be one ball in the bag. The probability of choosing a brown ball is 1 out of 18. Therefore, the probability of not choosing a brown ball is 17 out of 18 and the probability of having not a brown ball after removing 17 balls is the same.

8) **Choice C is correct**

   $\frac{1.75}{1.25} = 1.40 = 140\%$

9) **Choice B is correct**

   $\frac{450}{600} = 0.75 = 75\%$
   450 is 75% of 600. Therefore, the discount is: $100\% - 75\% = 25\%$

10) **Choice C is correct**

    $A = \frac{1}{2}bh,\ A = \frac{1}{2}(28)(9) = 126$

11) Choice A is correct

All angles in a triangle sum up to 180 degrees. Then: $51 + 47 = 98$, $180 - 98 = 82$

12) Choice D is correct

$P = 2(x + y), A = x.y, P = 2(x + y) \rightarrow 120 = 2(24 + y) \rightarrow 120 = 48 + 2y \rightarrow 72 = 2y \rightarrow y = 36, A = 24 \times 36 = 864$

13) Choice D is correct.

The distance that Mike runs can be found by the following equation: $D_M = 5.5t + 7.5$

The distance Julia runs can be found by $D_J = 6t$, Julia catches Mike if they run the same distance. Therefore, $6t = 5.5t + 7.5, 0.5t = 7.5 \rightarrow t = \frac{7.5}{0.5} = 15 \ hours$

14) Choice B is correct

Since Julie gives 8 pieces of candy to each of her friends, then, then number of pieces of candies must be divisible by 8.

A. $187 \div 8 = 23.375$
B. $216 \div 8 = 27$
C. $243 \div 8 = 30.375$
D. $223 \div 8 = 27.875$

Only choice B gives a whole number.

15) Choice C is correct

$\$9 \times 10 = \$90$, Petrol use: $10 \times 2 = 20$ liters, Petrol cost: $20 \times \$1 = \$20$

Money earned: $\$90 - \$20 = \$70$

16) Choice C is correct

$0.025 \times 100 = 2.5\%$

17) Choice B is correct

$\frac{4}{100} = 0.04$

18) Choice D is correct

If the length of the box is 27, then the width of the box is one third of it, 9, and the height of the box is 3 (one third of the width). The volume of the box is:

$V = (length)(width)(height) = (27)(9)(3) = 729 m^3$

19) Choice D is correct.

5 Full Length ISEE Lower Level Math Practice Tests

The failing rate is 25 out of $125 = \frac{25}{125}$, Change the fraction to percent: $\frac{25}{125} \times 100\% = 20\%$

20 percent of students failed. Therefore, 80 percent of students passed the exam.

20) Choice C is correct

    37 hr. 25 min.
    23 hr. 38 min.
    13 hr. 47 min.

21) Choice A is correct

An obtuse angle is an angle of greater than 90 degrees and less than 180 degrees. Only choice A is an obtuse angle.

22) Choice A is correct

$\frac{x+10+15+13+6}{5} = 10 \rightarrow x + 44 = 50 \quad \rightarrow \quad x = 50 - 44 = 6$

23) Choice D is correct.

There are 10 squares and 6 of them are shaded. Therefore, 6 out of 10 or $\frac{6}{10} = \frac{3}{5}$ are shaded.

24) Choice B is correct

Write a proportion and solve. $\frac{3}{2} = \frac{x}{90}$, Use cross multiplication: $2x = 270 \rightarrow x = 135$

25) Choice D is correct

To find the discount, multiply the number by $(100\% - rate\ of\ discount)$.

Therefore, for the first discount we get: $(200)(100\% - 25\%) = (200)(0.75)$

For the next 15% discount: $(200)(0.75)(0.85)$

26) Choice D is correct.

A quadrilateral with one pair of parallel sides is a trapezoid.

27) Choice A is correct.

Plug in 20 for A in the equations. Only option A works. $A + 20 = 40$, $20 + 20 = 40$

28) Choice D is correct

$1\ hour$: $\$3.75$, $8\ hours$: $8 \times \$3.75 = \$30$

29) Choice C is correct.

There are 54 students in the class. 18 of the are male and 36 of them are female. 36 out of 54 are female. Then: $\frac{36}{54} = \frac{x}{100} \rightarrow 3,600 = 54x \rightarrow x = 3,600 \div 54 \approx 67\%$

30) Choice B is correct.

1 pizza has 8 slices. 19 pizzas contain (19×8) 152 slices.

ISEE Lower Level Practice Test 4 Explanations
Quantitative Reasoning

1) **Choice D is correct.**
$\frac{8}{2} - \frac{3}{2} = \frac{5}{2} = 2.5$

2) **Choice B is correct.**
$48 = 3 \times N + 12 \rightarrow 3N = 48 - 12 = 36 \rightarrow N = 12$

3) **Choice C is correct.**
$7 + (4 \times N) = 23 \rightarrow 4N + 7 = 23$

4) **Choice D is correct.**

78 divided by 5, the remainder is 3. 45 divided by 7, the remainder is also 3.

5) **Choice A is correct.**

$3,400 - 606 = 2,794$

6) **Choice C is correct.**

All angles in a triangle sum up to 180 degrees. The triangle provided is an isosceles triangle. In an isosceles triangle, the three angles are 45, 45, and 90 degrees. Therefore, the value of x is 45.

7) **Choice B is correct.**

$4 \ percent \ of \ 480 = \frac{4}{100} \times 480 = \frac{1}{25} \times 480 = \frac{480}{25} = 19.2$

8) **Choice B is correct.**
The ratio of red marbles to blue marbles is 3 to 2. Therefore, the total number of marbles must be divisible by 5. $3 + 2 = 5$, 32 is the only one that is not divisible by 5.

9) **Choice D is correct.**
$Area \ of \ a \ square \ = \ side \times side = 81 \rightarrow side = 9$
$Perimeter \ of \ a \ square \ = \ 4 \times side \ = \ 4 \times 9 = 36$

10) **Choice B is correct.**
$5 + 3 = 8, \quad 8 + 4 = 12, \ 12 + 5 = 17 \ , \ 17 + 6 = 23$

11) Choice D is correct.

The length of the rectangle is 18. Then, its width is 6. $18 \div 3 = 6$

$Perimeter\ of\ a\ rectangle = 2 \times width + 2 \times length = 2 \times 6 + 2 \times 18 = 12 + 36 = 48$

12) Choice C is correct.

$Mary's\ Money = y, John's\ Money = y + 9, John\ gives\ Mary\ \$12 \rightarrow y + 9 - 12 = y - 3$

13) Choice D is correct.

Dividing 107 by 6 leaves a remainder of 5.

14) Choice C is correct.

$4,000 + A - 200 = 7,400 \rightarrow 4,000 + A = 7,400 + 200 = 7,600 \rightarrow A = 7,600 - 4,000 = 3,600$

15) Choice D is correct.

$75 off is the same as 15 percent off. Thus, 15 percent of a number is 75.

Then: $15\%\ of\ x = 75 \rightarrow 0.15x = 75 \rightarrow x = \frac{75}{0.15} = 500$

16) Choice A is correct.

$\frac{3}{2} = 1.5 > 1.4$

17) Choice A is correct.

$x + 5 = 6 \rightarrow x = 1, 2y = 8 \rightarrow y = 4, y - x = 4 - 1 = 3$

18) Choice C is correct.

$310 - x + 114 = 225 \rightarrow 310 - x = 225 - 114 = 111 \rightarrow x = 310 - 111 = 199$

19) Choice C is correct.

25 percent of $44.00 is $11. (Remember that 25 percent is equal to one fourth)

20) Choice C is correct.

$8.08 - 5.6 = 2.48$

21) Choice D is correct.

$500 + \square - 180 = 1,100 \rightarrow 500 + \square = 1,100 + 180 = 1,280, \square = 1,280 - 500 = 780$

22) Choice D is correct.

$\frac{1}{6}$ of students are girls. Therefore, $\frac{5}{6}$ of students in the class are boys. $\frac{5}{6}$ of 60 is 50. There are 50 boys in the class. $\frac{5}{6} \times 60 = \frac{300}{6} = 50$

23) Choice A is correct.

$N \times (5 - 3) = 12 \rightarrow N \times 2 = 12 \rightarrow N = 6$

24) Choice C is correct.

If $x ■ y = 3x + y - 2$, Then: $4 ■ 12 = 3(4) + 12 - 2 = 12 + 12 - 2 = 22$

25) Choice C is correct.
Of the numbers provided, 0.8923 is the greatest.

26) Choice A is correct.
$$\frac{7}{8} - \frac{3}{4} = \frac{7}{8} - \frac{6}{8} = \frac{1}{8} = 0.125$$

27) Choice A is correct.
The closest number to 4.02 is 4.

28) Choice D is correct.
$14 \div (2 + 5) = 14 \div 7 = 2$ is not 5

29) Choice B is correct

$240 + 45 = 285$

30) Choice D is correct
Let's order number of shirts sold per month: 130, 140, 145, 150, 160, 170
median is: $\frac{145+150}{2} = 147.5$

31) Choice D is correct

$180 \div 20 = 9$

32) Choice B is correct

$Speed = \frac{distance}{time}, 68 = \frac{2,600}{time} \rightarrow time = \frac{2,600}{68} = 38.23$

33) Choice C is correct

$\frac{13}{25} = 0.52$

34) Choice B is correct

$12a + 20 = 140, 12a = 140 - 20, 12a = 120, a = 10$

35) Choice B is correct

Thousandths

36) Choice D is correct

9 is NOT a prime factor. (it is divisible 3)

37) Choice C is correct

$\frac{85}{1,000} = 0.085$

38) Choice D is correct

$\frac{1}{2}$ of 26 hours is 13 hours. $\frac{1}{2} \times 26 = \frac{26}{2} = 13$

ISEE Lower Level Practice Test 4 Explanations
MATHEMATICS ACHIVEMENT

1) **Choice B is correct**

   $\{29, 24, 19, 14, 9\}$

2) **Choice B is correct**

   The factors of 18 are: $\{1, 2, 3, 6, 9, 18\}$, The factors of 32 are: $\{1, 2, 4, 8, 16, 32\}$, $GCF = 2$

3) **Choice A is correct**

   A. $\frac{12}{5} = 2.4$, B. $\frac{30}{5} = 6$, C. $\frac{15}{5} = 3$, D. $\frac{20}{5} = 4$

   Only choice A is not a multiple of 5.

4) **Choice C is correct**

   The perimeter of the triangle is: $6 + 8 + 10 = 24$

5) **Choice D is correct**

   The name of a rectangle with sides of equal length is square.

6) **Choice C is correct.**

   The question is that number 56,853.21 is how many times of number 5.685321. The answer is 10,000.

7) **Choice B is correct.**

   $\frac{3}{11}$ means 3 is divided by 11. The fraction line simply means division or $\div$. Therefore, we can write $\frac{3}{11}$ as $3 \div 11$.

8) **Choice C is correct.**

   Lily eats 2 pancakes in 1 minute $\Rightarrow$ Lily eats 3×5 pancakes in 5 minutes.

   Ella eats $2\frac{1}{4}$ pancakes in 1 minute $\Rightarrow$ Ella eats $2\frac{1}{4} \times 5$ pancakes in 5 minutes.

In total Lily and Ella eat $15 + 11.25$ pancakes in 5 minutes.

9) **Choice A is correct.**

   Simplify each option provided using order of operations rules.

   A. $8 - (-2) + (-18) = 8 + 2 - 18 = -8$
   B. $2 + (-3) \times (-2) = 2 + 6 = 8$
   C. $-6 \times (-6) + (-2) \times (-12) = 36 + 24 = 60$
   D. $(-2) \times (-7) + 4 = 14 + 4 = 18$

   Only option A is -8.

10) **Choice C is correct**

    $0.87 + 1.4 + 3.23 = 5.5$

11) **Choice C is correct**

    Perimeter of a rectangle $= 2(l + w) = 2(8 + 5) = 26$

12) **Choice D is correct**

    To solve this problem, divide $6\frac{1}{2}$ by $\frac{1}{4}$. $6\frac{1}{2} \div \frac{1}{4} = \frac{13}{2} \div \frac{1}{4} = \frac{13}{2} \times \frac{4}{1} = 26$

13) **Choice C is correct.**

    The clock shows the time 2:15 AM. 6 hours before that was 8:15 PM and 30 minutes before that was 7:45 PM.

14) **Choice B is correct.**

    $Area = w \times h, Area = 72, W = 8, 72 = 8 \times h, h = \frac{72}{8} = 9$

15) **Choice C is correct.**

    $25,980 \leq 28,097 \leq 29,207 \leq 30,700$

16) **Choice B is correct.**

    Low temperature is 24°F cooler than the temperature at 12: 00 *PM* that is 76°F, that means low temperature is 52°F (76°F − 24°F).

17) **Choice D is correct**

    $(5 + 7) \div (3^2 \div 2) = (12) \div (6 \div 2) = (12) \div (3) = 4$

18) Choice D is correct

$2.26 + 14.69 + 2.50 + 4.66 + 17.99 = 42.1$

19) Choice D is correct

$1 - (-8) = 1 + 8 = 9$

20) Choice A is correct.

Add number of all students to know the whole number of students. $86 + 32 = 118$

21) Choice A is correct.

$\frac{11}{19} \cong 0.579$

22) Choice D is correct.

$80 \times 34 = 2,720$

23) Choice C is correct.

The first picture is divided to 16 parts that 6 parts of it is shaded ($\frac{6}{16}$). The second picture is divided to 10 parts that 5 parts of that is shaded ($\frac{5}{10}$).

24) Choice C is correct.

The digit 6 has a value of $6 \times \frac{1}{100}$, The digit 4 has a value of $4 \times 10,000$, The digit 5 has a value of $5 \times 1,000$.

25) Choice B is correct.

Three – digit odd numbers that have a 5 in the hundreds place and a 2 in the tens place are $521, 523, 525, 527, 529.$ 527 is one of alternatives.

26) Choice B is correct

$average\ (mean) = \frac{sum\ of\ terms}{number\ of\ terms} = \frac{9+12+15+16+19+16+14.5}{7} = 14.5$

27) Choice A is correct

$probability = \frac{desired\ outcomes}{possible\ outcomes} = \frac{4}{4+3+7+10} = \frac{4}{24} = \frac{1}{6}$

28) Choice D is correct.

0.62 is equal to $\frac{62}{100}$

29) Choice B is correct.

Find the least common denominator (LCD), then rewriting each term as an equivalent fraction with the LCD. Then we compare the numerators of each fraction and put them in correct order from least to greatest or greatest to least. LCD of 2, 8, 4 and 16 is 16. Rewrite the input fractions as equivalent fractions using the LCD:

A. $\frac{8}{16}$ B. $\frac{6}{16}$ C. $\frac{12}{16}$ B. $\frac{9}{16}$

So choice B has the least value.

30) Choice D is correct.

$1\ year = 365\ days, 1\ day = 24\ hours, 1\ year = 365 \times 24, 1\ year = 8{,}760$

ISEE Lower Level Practice Test 5

Quantitative Reasoning

1) **Choice B is correct.**
$$\frac{10}{4} - \frac{3}{4} = \frac{7}{4} = 1.75$$

2) **Choice B is correct.**
$68 = 4 \times N + 12 \rightarrow 4 \times N = 68 - 12 = 56 \rightarrow N = 14$

3) **Choice C is correct.**
Four times a number N is $6 \times N$. When 5 is added to it, the result is: $5 + (6 \times N) = 27 \rightarrow 6N + 5 = 27$

4) **Choice D is correct.**
58 divided by 5, the remainder is 3. 66 divided by 7, the remainder is also 3.

5) **Choice A is correct.**

$3{,}600 - 707 = 2{,}893$

6) **Choice C is correct.**

All angles in a triangle sum up to 180 degrees. The triangle provided is an isosceles triangle. In an isosceles triangle, the three angles are 45, 45, and 90 degrees. Therefore, the value of x is 45.

7) **Choice B is correct.**

$5\ percent\ of\ 360 = \dfrac{5}{100} \times 580 = \dfrac{1}{20} \times 580 = \dfrac{580}{20} = 29$

8) **Choice B is correct.**
   The ratio of red marbles to blue marbles is 1 to 5. Therefore, the total number of marbles must be divisible by 6. $5 + 1 = 6$, 26 is the only one that is not divisible by 6.

9) **Choice B is correct.**
   $Area\ of\ a\ square = side \times side = 49 \rightarrow side = 7$
   $Perimeter\ of\ a\ square = 4 \times side = 4 \times 7 = 28$

10) **Choice B is correct.**
    $6 + 3 = 9,\quad 9 + 4 = 13,\ 13 + 5 = 18\ ,\ 18 + 6 = 24$

11) **Choice D is correct.**
    The length of the rectangle is 27. Then, its width is 9. $27 \div 3 = 9$
    $$Perimeter\ of\ a\ rectangle = 2 \times width + 2 \times length = 2 \times 9 + 2 \times 27 = 18 + 54 = 72$$

12) **Choice C is correct.**

$Mary's\ Money = y, John's\ Money = y + 11, John\ gives\ Mary\ \$14 \rightarrow y + 11 - 14 = y - 3$

13) **Choice D is correct.**

    Dividing 108 by 5 leaves a remainder of 3.

14) **Choice C is correct.**
    $$5,000 + A - 300 = 8,400 \rightarrow 5,000 + A = 8,400 + 300 = 8,700 \rightarrow A = 8,700 - 5,000 = 3,700$$

15) **Choice D is correct.**

    $90 off is the same as 25 percent off. Thus, 25 percent of a number is 90.

    Then: $25\%\ of\ x = 90 \rightarrow 0.25x = 90 \rightarrow x = \dfrac{90}{0.25} = 360$

16) **Choice A is correct.**

    $\dfrac{7}{4} = 1.4$, the only choice provided that is less than 1.4 is choice A. $\dfrac{7}{5} = 1.4 > 1.2$

17) **Choice B is correct.**
    $x + 4 = 6 \rightarrow x = 2, 2y = 10 \rightarrow y = 5, y - x = 5 - 2 = 3$

18) **Choice C is correct.**
    $320 - x + 116 = 235 \rightarrow 320 - x = 235 - 116 = 119 \rightarrow x = 320 - 119 = 201$

19) **Choice C is correct.**
    25 percent of $64.00 is $16. (Remember that 25 percent is equal to one fourth)

20) **Choice D is correct.**

    $8.08 - 4.6 = 3.48$

21) Choice D is correct.

$700 + \square - 180 = 1,300 \rightarrow 700 + \square = 1,300 + 180 = 1,480, \square = 1,480 - 700 = 780$

22) Choice D is correct.

$\frac{1}{5}$ of students are girls. Therefore, $\frac{4}{5}$ of students in the class are boys. $\frac{4}{5}$ of 65 is 52. There are 52 boys in the class. $\frac{4}{5} \times 65 = \frac{260}{5} = 52$

23) Choice A is correct.

$N \times (6 - 4) = 18 \rightarrow N \times 2 = 18 \rightarrow N = 9$

24) Choice C is correct.

If $x \blacksquare y = 4x + y - 2$, Then: $5 \blacksquare 20 = 4(5) + 20 - 2 = 20 + 20 - 2 = 38$

25) Choice C is correct.

Of the numbers provided, 0.6923 is the greatest.

26) Choice B is correct.

$\frac{10}{8} - \frac{3}{4} = \frac{10}{8} - \frac{6}{8} = \frac{4}{8} = 0.5$

27) Choice A is correct.

The closest number to 7.02 is 7.

28) Choice D is correct.

$15 \div (2 + 3) = 15 \div 5 = 3$ is not 4

29) Choice B is correct

$275 + 35 = 310$

30) Choice B is correct

In the choices provided the only whole number greater than 44 is 440. Other numbers are not whole numbers greater than 44.

31) Choice D is correct

$186 \div 31 = 6$

32) Choice B is correct

$Speed = \frac{distance}{time}, 50 = \frac{3,500}{time} \rightarrow time = \frac{3,500}{50} = 70$, It takes Nicole about 70 hours to go from city A to city B.

33) Choice C is correct

$\frac{4}{25} = 0.16$

34) Choice B is correct

$10a + 30 = 150, 10a = 150 - 30, 10a = 120, a = 12$

35) Choice B is correct

the place value of 4 in 7.7345 is thousandths.

36) Choice D is correct

6 is NOT a prime factor. (it is divisible by 2 and 3)

37) Choice C is correct

$$\frac{45}{1,000} = 0.045$$

38) Choice D is correct

$\frac{1}{8}$ of 24 hours is 3 hours. $\frac{1}{8} \times 24 = \frac{24}{8} = 3$

ISEE Lower Level Practice Test 5
Mathematics Achievement

1) Choice A is correct

Sixty-five thousand, eight hundred nineteen is written as 65,819.

2) Choice C is correct

The greatest common factor of 22 and 32 is 2.

3) Choice A is correct

From choices provided, only 10 is NOT a multiple of 6.

4) Choice C is correct

The perimeter of the triangle is: $5 + 4 + 3 = 12$

5) Choice D is correct

3,666 divided by 6 is 611.

6) Choice C is correct.

The question is that number 46,743.21 is how many times of number 4.674321. The answer is 10,000.

7) Choice B is correct.

$\frac{7}{11}$ means 7 is divided by 11. The fraction line simply means division or ÷. Therefore, we can write $\frac{7}{11}$ as $7 \div 11$.

8) Choice C is correct.

Lily eats 2 pancakes in 1 minute ⇒ Lily eats 2×5 pancakes in 5 minutes.

Ella eats $2\frac{1}{2}$ pancakes in 1 minute ⇒ Ella eats $2\frac{1}{2} \times 5$ pancakes in 5 minutes.

In total Lily and Ella eat $10 + 12.5 = 22.5$ pancakes in 5 minutes.

9) Choice B is correct.

Simplify each choice provided using order of operations rules.

A. $8 - (-2) + (-18) = 8 + 2 - 18 = -8$
B. $2 + (-3) \times (-2) = 2 + 6 = 8$
C. $-6 \times (-6) + (-2) \times (-12) = 36 + 24 = 60$
D. $(-2) \times (-7) + 4 = 14 + 4 = 18$

Only choice B is 8.

10) Choice C is correct

$0.97 + 1.6 + 4.23 = 6.8$

11) Choice B is correct

$Perimeter\ of\ a\ rectangle = 2(length + width) = 2(6 + 7) = 26$

12) Choice D is correct

To solve this problem, divide $6\frac{1}{2}$ by $\frac{1}{8}$. $6\frac{1}{2} \div \frac{1}{8} = \frac{13}{2} \div \frac{1}{8} = \frac{13}{2} \times \frac{8}{1} = 52$

13) Choice C is correct.

$\frac{16}{24} = \frac{2}{3}$

14) Choice B is correct.

$Area = width \times height,\ Area = 63,\ Width = 9,\ 63 = 9 \times height,\ height = \frac{63}{9} = 7$

15) Choice C is correct.

$55.09 - 12.34 = 42.75$

16) Choice B is correct.

Low temperature is 35°F cooler than the temperature at 12:00 PM that is 87°F, that means low temperature is 52°F (87°F − 35°F).

17) Choice C is correct

$(12 + 4) \div (4^2 \div 2) = (12) \div (16 \div 2) = (16) \div (8) = 2$

18) Choice D is correct

$4.26 + 16.69 + 2.50 + 4.66 + 17.99 = 46.1$

19) Choice D is correct

The line is from −1 to −10. So it is 9 units.

20) Choice A is correct.

To find total number of students in Riddle Elementary school, add number of all students.

$97 + 33 = 130$

21) Choice A is correct.

$\frac{13}{20} = 0.65$

22) Choice D is correct.

$90 \times 46 = 4,140$

23) Choice C is correct.

___ $+ 12 − 8 = 55$. Then, the missing number is 51.

$$51 + 12 − 8 = 55$$

24) Choice C is correct.

The digit 6 has a value of $5 \times \frac{1}{100}$, The digit 4 has a value of $4 \times 10,000$, The digit 8 has a value of $8 \times 10 = 800$, The digit 5 has a value of $9 \times 1,000$.

25) Choice B is correct.

Three − digit odd numbers that have a 6 in the hundreds place and a 3 in the tens place are 631, 633, 635, 637, 639. 637 is one of the choices.

26) Choice B is correct

$$average\ (mean) = \frac{sum\ of\ terms}{number\ of\ terms} = \frac{7+11+13.5+16+19+16+14.5}{7} = 13.85$$

27) Choice B is correct

$$probability = \frac{desired\ outcomes}{possible\ outcomes} = \frac{3}{4+3+8+9} = \frac{3}{24} = \frac{1}{8}$$

28) Choice C is correct.

0.92 is equal to $\frac{92}{100}$

29) Choice B is correct.

From the fractions provided $\frac{3}{8}$ has the least value.

30) Choice D is correct.

$$Volume\ of\ a\ box = width \times length \times height = 4 \times 5 \times 3 = 60$$

"Effortless Math" Publications

Effortless Math authors' team strives to prepare and publish the best quality Mathematics learning resources to make learning Math easier for all. We hope that our publications help you or your student Math in an effective way.

We all in Effortless Math wish you good luck and successful studies!

Effortless Math Authors

www.EffortlessMath.com

... So Much More Online!

- ✓ FREE Math lessons

- ✓ More Math learning books!

- ✓ Mathematics Worksheets

- ✓ Online Math Tutors

Need a PDF version of this book?

Visit www.EffortlessMath.com

Made in the USA
Columbia, SC
01 November 2019